CONTENTS

The purpose of this 'diary'?

A book for working mums/dads, at home mums/dads, gonna be mums/dads, anyone's mum/dad, somebody's mum/dad, everybody's mum/dad! As the years have flown by, I have had the pleasure of getting to know all the mums and dads mentioned above.

I salute all parents for all they are and all they do. I learned some very important life lessons from mine, and this book is dedicated to them:

My Warriors of Substance...

my mum... *Ann Florence Olliver*

and dad.... *Cecil Julian Olliver* ... I miss you still!

...my husband...Luke.. this would not have happened without you!

...my children...Brendt, Rebecca and Kimberley... you gave me loads of material!

From my desk.... In a profession like teaching, we are dealing with children who are not our own and yet...they are! They are our class, our girls, our boys, our responsibility...OUR children.

There are anywhere between 16-60 children in a class, depending on geographic, economic and demographic factors. So, at any given time, a single teacher will need to be able to impact multiple minds. This individual will also need to challenge those who can be, encourage and support those who need it, while not forgetting everyone else, the core of the class. Now add behaviour to the class dynamic... and to that self-esteem, confidence, and other social skills... and now you have... a CIRCUS!!

A juggler juggles, on an average, between 8-10 items in one act... one performance. A teacher does this every day for 7-8 hours straight!!

Kudos to you, my fellow jugglers... caregivers, super folk, bodyguards, cuddle-givers, 'time out' dispensers, walking encyclopedias... TEACHERS!!

'May the words of my mouth and the meditations of my heart be pleasing in your sight, O Lord, My Rock and My Redeemer'.

– Psalm 19:14

Why the name Periwinkle?

It symbolises new beginnings and new friendships.

I hope this book is the beginning of many friendly chats, with cups of tea or coffee and always with lots of love.

Warm wishes and hugs,
Periwinkle

The Contents

Dear Diary,

I once had someone ask me a question: **"How long will my child take to settle in school?"** That is actually a very difficult question for any teacher to answer. There's no wrong answer, really... just answers that can prove to be wrong.

It is always a dilemma for a teacher to know what to say, as there are two sides to this question- 'settle down' and 'how long'. These could be due to a variety of reasons: too many moves, too many different schools, too many days off from school, family changes (loss, divorce, re-marriage) and a variety of other things.

The more appropriate thing to do would be to give the teacher your child's background... history, if you like—and say with a smile, "Let me know if I can support you to help my child settle in."

I remember, at a meeting with one particular set of parents, the child was taking a while to mix with the other children. Being Grade One made things easier, or so I thought!

I asked the parents to come in (being new to the school). I wanted to get to know them and get a better idea of their little one. They told me that they had been victims of an armed home robbery in Europe. In fact, their child had had a gun pointed at their head! The trauma had passed with counselling and visits to a clinical psychologist. With the move to Dubai, the anxiety, lack of confidence, fear of water, vomiting, etc., had started again. In short, the symptoms had returned.

I was at a complete loss at what to say or do to put their minds at rest.

Their honest revelation helped me understand the child's unfounded fear and anxiety about trying anything new.

I remembered what my mother had always told me... a child can sense a parent's anxiety. Even if the parent shows no apparent signs of this, manifestations begin to show in their child.

I soon realised what a difficult time the mother and father were going through. They were blaming themselves and were trying to bottle up their feelings. After a long, honest chat, what they took away from that meeting, and indeed all parents should know... be calm and tell your child the truth as you see it.

Here are a few sentences I keep in my back pocket... just in case:

> *"Yes, I know how you feel." "I am here for you."*
> *"Whatever you are feeling is perfectly alright for now."*

(In the case of vomiting) *"Your tummy is such a sensible tummy... it throws out anything that it knows is not good for your body."*

(In case of fear of water) *"Only try to put your toes in today. Tomorrow is a new day, and you can try to put your knees in, too."*

Anxiety is a negative, detrimental emotional force that can claim precedence over every other feeling.

Anticipation is a positive, emotional force that can be unlocked to counter the effects of anxiety.

Here are a few tips...to help with the 'What Ifs' your child may have...

What If ... I am anxious about a first time activity, health, life, etc., mummy?

- Anticipate that it will be unlike any other experience.

- Embrace the fact that someone else is in charge, and all you can do, is follow every instruction the best that you can.

- Understand that the 'ball truly is in your court'...do YOUR BEST as well as you can.

- As the saying goes...Put your best foot forward! All the footsteps that follow will be just as good!

So... to come back to settling into school... nobody can honestly put a time limit on that. It depends on school and home being in sync, in tandem with each other. One can't function effectively without the other. The most anyone can do is try to make each experience as rewarding as possible for the child.

To experience any sort of success, one has to <u>decide that one is capable of succeeding!</u>

There is no substitute for hard work and perseverance. Both these have to be instilled as positive character traits that continue to develop and be nurtured as a child grows; in fact, adults would do well to demonstrate them! They never go out of style and are always fashionable!

Suffice it to say that the little child in this diary entry has since become a confident, perseverant, self-assured young person with an inquiring mind and not afraid to try something for the first time!

Yes, my grin spreads from ear to ear. **SUCCESS!!!** They had decided they were capable of success and so had I!

**Warm wishes and hugs,
Periwinkle**

Dear Diary,

Somebody once asked me, **"What do you consider the most important thing we should give our children?"** I am no expert on life or philosophy. I wouldn't even know where to start on the subject! BUT... I do know children, and yes... I could go on and on about *that* subject!

After having a think about it, I would say **stability**... that would be my answer.

It is the right of every child on this planet! As parents, we must all work hard to provide this to our children. It would require us to be very strong, emotionally, and mentally. It is very difficult to be completely consistent all the time. Mood swings are a luxury that we do not indulge in. Unless, by some twist of fate, we have been unable to do this... ASK FOR HELP!! Do NOT negotiate your child's peace of mind or your own—**no matter what.**

At some point in their lifetime, every parent has wondered about their child's social behaviour at school.

The diagram shows that home is all-encompassing for a child's state; emotional, social and mental preparedness starts at the outermost circle and permeates inward.

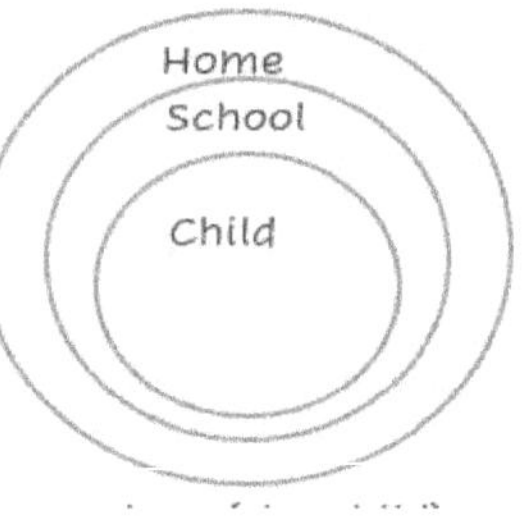

atmosphere x shell = behaviour of the nucleus
(home) x (school) = (the child)

A strong, sustained, and positive relationship needs to be initiated and then maintained. As parents, we have our children's best interests at heart—so do their teachers!

Recently, there was an incident of bullying. A child was being bullied on a regular basis at school. It was not physical, but verbal and emotional bullying and was getting to the point where the child was dreading school. The class teacher had no idea about the situation because this would not happen in her lessons. The parent of the child happened to be a teacher in the school.

Normally, parents would write a note or email or meet the teacher for a quick word, or in extreme cases of 'do good' sense, speak to the child concerned directly (not acceptable, by the way). This mum felt the need to go to her colleague without an appointment, barge into her classroom and 'have a word'. Being quite unaware of the incident, the teacher did not appreciate the intrusion. Nobody likes to be 'on the back foot', and she was no exception. Hence, instead of it being a positive and helpful interaction, the rendezvous became defensive and strained. Of course, being the consummate professional, the teacher assured the mother of an investigation (which happened promptly), but there was a sense that, somehow, the professional trust that had built up over the term had been broken.

You see, by going to see her unannounced, the teacher must have felt that the mum had not given her a chance to gather some facts about the incident and had managed to make her feel inadequate as a professional. Nobody, no matter what they do, should feel that way or be made to feel that way. It is debilitating to their morale and sense of self-worth.

Though the parent intended to safeguard her child, she ended up being the bully that she was demanding needed.

To be addressed. In due course, the teacher was able to address the issue, and the situation was sorted out. However, the mother soon realised what it felt like when a similar incident happened in her own classroom.

She sent the teacher a scented candle and a note to apologise for her insensitivity. All is well though, I am happy to report, as teachers we are always willing to give 'truants' a million second chances.

What could have been done differently?

- Write a note or email <u>asking</u> (not demanding or accusing) if the teacher has noticed what your child has told you. This need not be restricted to bullying; they are a good way to deal with most incidents.

- Give the teacher <u>time</u> to investigate, take the necessary action, and give you her feedback. <u>Wait</u> for her reply.

If the situation continues then other steps can be taken to resolve the situation. Remember the diagram?

Courtesy is caught, and you are the carrier...
make the time for a little courtesy... it will go a
long way!

– 21 –

Warm wishes and hugs,
Periwinkle

Dear Diary,

I have never been very lucky with coin flips, jackpot machines, Bingo or most other games of chance. But...I have been very fortunate in that I have been part of many 'coin flips' as far as the children in my class go.

There are people who think that a teacher is as good as the class she influences. But I think it goes far beyond that. To say the above is to judge a human being, who may or may not have a strong impact on every single mind he/she encounters. That is not to say there is no impact at all ... just different levels of it.

Just like with our own children, our impact as parents may not have the same result on each of our children, but... there is an impact, nonetheless. What is most important is that we need to make sure the impact we make proceeds to build up rather than the opposite.

Over the years, I have had the good fortune to talk to many parents about how they prepare their children for a new school, class, year, etc. I have found that, by and large, most parents have the right idea...you know, the usual **"school will be such fun"** or **"you will make many new friends."**

Being the new kid on the block is daunting, to say the least. So, give your child a strong sense of who they are no matter which school they go to. That is not to say give them insolence, arrogance, or conceit... but it does mean you show by example the importance of respect, empathy, and, most of all, tools to resolve conflict.

The saying **'Those who can't do ...teach'**... is the most idiotic statement I have ever heard, but unfortunately, many people agree with it. Again, impact! Words have an impact and not just on one life. A ripple effect is created and grows and grows, touching minds and hearts and, in this case, causing disrespect to flourish.

Teachers are the most misunderstood bunch of people on the planet! Parents are also the most misunderstood bunch of people on the planet. Both groups have 'by and large' one very important trait in common: They care about their 'brood' of children... unconditionally. My class... my kids... phrases that lead one to believe that their impact is inevitable... and it is. Sadly, it is not always to the benefit of the child.

Another way they are inextricably connected is in the 'blame game'! If a child behaves in an unpleasant manner, the teacher invariably blames the parent... and not to be outdone; if this happens at home, the parents blame bad teaching. The fact is, we go back to the diagram in the book... we are all responsible.

Yes, believe it or not, but 'bad' behaviour, though it begins (in many cases) at home, it flourishes in a conducive environment, which includes school too!

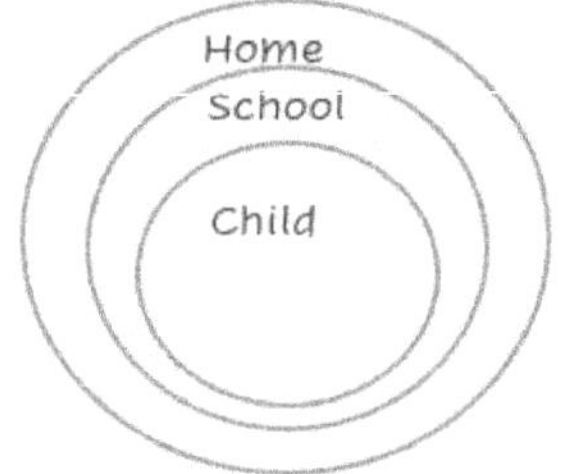

Periwinkle's Magic List: the 5 M's

- **Model:** model the behaviour you want from day 1; you are the best example for your child/class.

- **Manage:** manage situations to allow the child to imitate and respond to what you have been modelling.

- **Monitor:** watch from the sidelines, don't be intrusive, allow the child some 'room'.

- **Manifest:** give situations for learned skills to be used/shown (manifested).

- **Motivate:** reward good behaviour; praise is a fantastic tool to use as a reward (rewards do not need to be monetary).

Repeat the 5 M's process:

Become the person who instils beauty in your children and enjoy the benefits:

- **A higher rate of success**

- Better cognitive development

- Well-balanced outlook on life and living

- Motivated young people to become good global citizens

- Deep conviction of self-worth and ability from a teacher and parent all-in-one... the **5M's** work...they are my secret weapon, so use them well.

All the very best, my co-conspirators!!

Warm wishes and hugs,
Periwinkle

Dear Diary,

"How come I can never be organised in the morning!" another question that I have been asked quite often by new mums, as I am seen as someone (being a teacher) who has some semblance of order to her life.

It is widely accepted that our morning routine sets the tone for our day. So, we make sure that from waking up to leaving for work, our time is tranquil and almost divinely well-organised. This is a fairly easy task for a single, working professional provided your alarm clock works, the phone is charged, clothes are ironed and ready, food is packed, etc. Let any one of these components 'malfunction'... then we have a recipe for a mad rush, crazy hair, wild eyes, a furrowed brow, uncoordinated movements...in short, disaster!

Then

optimal functionality + tranquility = good start to the day

Becomes

malfunction + zero tranquility = terrifying start to the day

Now multiply the situation with a spouse and children... the likelihood of equation 2 becoming a daily occurrence and equation 1 melting into oblivion... is a very real possibility. Have I scared you off? I hope not... I have a few tips to help ease out the creases and allow for some 'smooth sailing' so to speak.

Planning:

A plan is nothing; planning is everything. A plan is without merit if it is not followed, so organise your time effectively. Choose small tasks that can be accomplished easily with maximum benefit.

Example: Make a list of items you need from the store and get them delivered rather than going to the shop yourself. This gives you time to iron clothes, hang out laundry, load the washing machine, etc. This thing called 'time management' many of us find a challenge...I know I do!

Think of things that can be done simultaneously, e.g., Boiling eggs and packing school bags... we don't need to watch the egg!

Use a slow cooker to cook the food while you toast the bread for sandwiches, or get uniforms ready for school the next day.

Words Work!

I spoke about impact earlier in the book, and I repeat it... words have an impact.

Positive words = positive impact.

Choose a phrase to say that will lift you up. A starting point that will impact your day and allow you to experience beauty even in the little things.

"This will be a good day."

"It's good to be me, for I am fearfully and wonderfully made."

"I am awesome because God made me that way."

"What a beautiful morning it is."

Yesterday Vs Today

To have a stress-free today, we need a well-organised yesterday!

TO DO lists are a good idea....though if you are like me, then I need to find the list first!! Then...I am not sure if it is today's list or yesterday's since I forgot to date it!! So ...now I have come up with a new strategy that works well for me, and I hope it will work for you too!

My **Yesterday vs Today plan...**

Yesterday **Prep & Pack** (night before)	Today **Pick & Go** (morning)
-iron clothes -Pack bags (work & school) -clean shoes -pack extra kit (PE/gym) -lunch (cook, cool, pack) Total Time: 1-1 ½ hr	Wake up, wash, dress - 20mins Eat breakfast- 15mins Walk & Wave (pick up bags, lunch, keys etc. goodbyes) - 5 mins Total time: 40mins

These take planning. Be prepared to do a few 'test' runs before you find what works best for you and your household.

If your child/children are older, they do their own prep, and you check. This also takes repetition.

Ever heard of the phrase 'Practice makes Perfect'? That's all this is.

Warm wishes and hugs,
Periwinkle

Dear Diary,

Now...the next few happenings can derail even the most well-oiled engine so be aware... don't beware!

Parents have often asked me about a variety of things and any tips I might have for them... especially about **'getting ready for school'** times. I have chosen a few of the most common ones for this entry so it will be rather long... please bear with me!

"She/He never listens to me!"

Okay, let's be honest...never is a bit worrying! If a child consistently ignores a parent's words, there is something sad about that apart from being rather distressing, too!

An open ear is the only believable sign of an open heart.... you understand life as you learn to live- as you learn to listen. As a teacher, one's first reaction to a statement like this would be to say. **"But she always listens to me!"** Both words are extremes and hardly ever encompass the truth. So... what should we do?

Why does 'she' never <u>listen</u>? To make 'getting ready' times calmer, a good idea would be to be calm yourself. Children feed off our emotional and mental state... so you must master the art of outward calm even if your nerves are a jangled mess! You would have to be an exceptional actor to do this every day, no matter what. An easier solution is to have everything ready, so all you really have to do is spend time with your child, not at her! Depending on the age, help her get ready so that breakfast is not rushed. Also, there's no harm in a little 'bribery'... favourite breakfast cereal or snack for school to help lift the mood. Tiny gestures that don't cost much, but show that you care about your child's well-being.

Obedience and trust go together, and for very young children, trust is built with hugs, their favourite things and getting their way in some things (carry the car keys, wear a special hat to the school gate, etc.). A peaceful start to the day usually means a happy day... for everyone!

Of course, if the child is 5 years or older then, other positive measures work better than immediate gratification... **"If you are super sensible getting ready this morning, I will let your teacher know how trustworthy you are at home"...**

"Now look how well you brushed your teeth. I know you will be super quick getting dressed." **Nothing** like positive reinforcement! Have a few sentences like these in your repertoire, your **'go-to'** ammunition for sticky situations.

"He refuses to dress himself... and is 9 years old now!"

If this is a one-off tantrum then without condoning it, you can 'help' but try not to actually put the clothes on him.

If this has been happening for a while, and there is a stubborn refusal to do anything while dressing himself (the parent does everything), my advice to the parent was... **"Bring him to school as he is, in his pyjamas."** The parents were shocked! How could they do that? Very easily... let your child have breakfast...pick up his stuff, hold hands and walk to the car...seatbelts and drive to school (be sure to carry a spare uniform with you). When your child sees that the tantrum has not had the desired effect, it will cease to be of any value to him. You may need to repeat the exercise depending on your child.

Usually, the child will not want to walk into school without his uniform...this is when you park, give him a hug and politely inform him that the consequence for the tantrum is a school entry in pyjamas every day unless he decides to be a grown up young man and dress himself every morning. There is no need for harsh words, anger, or raised tones... the problem is solved. Chances are he will obey. Always remember to say you love him... **always!**

"My child won't eat breakfast on his own; he wants me to feed him.... and he can do it...he does it every day at dinnertime."

Depending on the age of the child, you would need to handle it differently, but always in a way that is loving but firm...

For very young children (aged 2-4 years), being fed is a very soothing exercise for them, and as a parent, one should not shy away from it. Your child is telling you that he/she likes that contact with you each morning to help them start their day... **enjoy it!** This will be easy if you have planned your day well and done the prep the night before.

For young children (aged 5-7 years), it could be that they just require reassurance, which can be given in a variety of ways:

- sensible sentences from your arsenal,

- 'help' with a few spoonfuls, then ask them to 'help' you by eating some on their own while you 'check' on something,

- make a 'deal' ... "I feed you three spoons, you feed yourself 3."

All these make it easier to wean them off the 'feeding'. Reward them with a hug or sticker, etc., for when they do it independently... make a BIG deal of their little victories.

Celebrate life with them. They won't be this age forever... plus celebrations never go out of style!

Warm wishes and hugs,
Periwinkle

Dear Diary,

I have always wondered about the benefits of rewards... is there such a thing as too many rewards?

Science says there is an equal and opposite reaction to every action.... something like that. Religions talk about 'karma'...the Bible clearly says', As you sow, so shall you reap'... in other words, one's choices and their consequences go together like peanut butter and jelly. So, where do rewards come in?

As a primary teacher, rewards are our magic wand, and they are used in almost every kind of situation. As a parent, rewards most often tend to be monetary... raised allowance, new toy, new game, new this, new that... who's to say when it gets too much? Even behavioural psychologists or animal trainers will tell you that rewards work well to entice appropriate behaviour.

A parent once asked me about this. Each time their son did even the smallest thing, like saying 'thank you', he would get a new toy or some kind of reward. So very soon, this child, let's say, Max, only displayed appropriate behaviour if there was a reward... the proverbial carrot being dangled. Of course, this strategy soon began to work in the opposite way and became 'bribery' instead.

As his teacher, I had to undo all that the well-meaning parents had done, and together, we began his 'feelings' journey. We began to show him the value of self-worth, pride in his effort, humility (he is still learning this one), thought before action, choices, and 'putting himself in others' shoes'.

I remember my first sentences to him were, **"Everyone in this room is special to me. I want you to show me what I already know is true about you."**

Always speak words of worth over your children. Tell them they are beautiful and wonderful, and I believe- blessings of God. Words have power, so use them wisely. If you say "You are a bad boy" to a child, chances are he will prove you right.

I remember an incident where the parents of a little boy in my Year 1 class came to see me at the Parent Teacher Conference. The dad was a jovial gentleman with a resounding laugh, while the mum was a lovely lady, mild, and a little shy. They were happy with their son's schoolwork.Then the father made a comment that I remember retaliating rather harshly to. He asked me how I was dealing with his 'naughty boy' and then laughed. My demeanour changed, and I curtly informed him that his little boy was NOT naughty, just active. He looked suitably surprised and a little uncomfortable; then mum spoke up... it came out that this little boy ran circles around his mum at home and rarely listened to her, and when she told his dad, the answer was always, "Well he is a naughty boy so that's what he will do, right Ellis?" I was not happy, to put it mildly. He was conditioning the child to behave in a certain way, even though at school, I could see that the opposite was the child's nature. He wasn't a 'naughty' boy at all. He just had trouble making sensible decisions and controlling himself sometimes.

I tried very hard to hold myself in check (you guys would have been very proud of me) and proceeded to ask if Mum would like things to change. She nodded vehemently, and Dad looked at her and then at me, very surprised. "You really think Ellis can behave differently?" I nodded. Any child can behave differently if that's what we imbue in them and show them;

they learn by watching. The first thing I told Dad he would have to do was stop calling Ellis a naughty boy. That had to stop ASAP! The next thing we agreed to do was give Ellis some non-negotiable ground rules at home, e.g. Walk in the kitchen, Eat with a spoon, Tidy up your toys, etc. Notice these are rules without the word NO. Ellis was also to have 30 minutes of running play every day, in their garden or at the park. The last thing I told them to do was to use the school diary to let me know how he was doing once every week, either on a Monday or Friday. To say the change in Ellis was significant is an understatement. That little boy went from downright boisterous to actively bearable in days. I wrote a note to the parents letting them know how well Ellis was doing, and Mum sent back a reply that I will always treasure... "If it hadn't been for you, our little Ellis would have never known the power of self-worth and pride in himself. We wouldn't have got to know what a wonderful boy we had; thank you, Miss."

Whether in jest or even in anger, check what you are saying... it is immensely difficult but is immensely important! Have a few 'angry sentences' that you can use rather than letting your anger get the better of you. I remember reading a poem in college about the tongue, and one of the lines said... ' **The tongue of man so small and weak, can crush and kill... declared the Greeks'**

How true is that! This is something I try to instil in my classroom and as a parent too.

With this particular child, I would make him rephrase his sentences till they went from downright rude to somewhat bearable! I also told his parents to do the same, and soon, he began using his words to express himself without damaging the self-esteem of his peers (or adults). The Bible also says...

'A gentle word turns away wrath, but a harsh word stirs up anger'

- Proverbs 15:1

Some of my 'angry' sentences are:

"I know you are upset, but a beautiful child like you needs to be more sensible with your... (words, actions, etc.)"

"This is very disappointing to see. I know how beautiful you are, now try and be more careful about ... next time."

"Excuse me! A child as wonderful as you should not be doing/saying things like this. What do you think you need to do/say next?"

A Chinese proverb wisely says... "A man who keeps his tongue keeps his soul."

There is always a lot to be said.... It all depends on how we say it.

Rewards are these amazing gems that we get to give to 'deserving' winners. Everyone on this earth wants to be appreciated ... the trick is to notice what they do so the rewards can be given in a timely manner, or else they lose their value and momentum.

Rewards can be verbal, an action, or a token.

Loving recognition for something important and worthy of notice.

Rewards must be like a **S T R E A M**...

S-special

T-timely

R-relevant

E-earned (deserved)

A-appropriate

M-meaningful

One can hardly reward a 'Thank you' with the latest gadgets! Yet a selfless act could warrant an hour's play at Magic Planet (gaming zone) or a day at the zoo etc. Keep it simple, keep it going, keep it consistent.

Be proactive, not reactive!

Children are blessings we as parents need to guide, nurture and love.

As mentioned earlier in the book, use the 5 M's and enjoy rewarding every milestone, every success and every lesson learned.

Warm wishes and hugs,
Periwinkle

Dear Diary,

"Miss, my child behaves so differently in your classroom than at home. What did you do?"

Now, I am no magician and would not be so presumptuous to assume that my classroom strategies always work, but ... let's just say I have seen a lot of

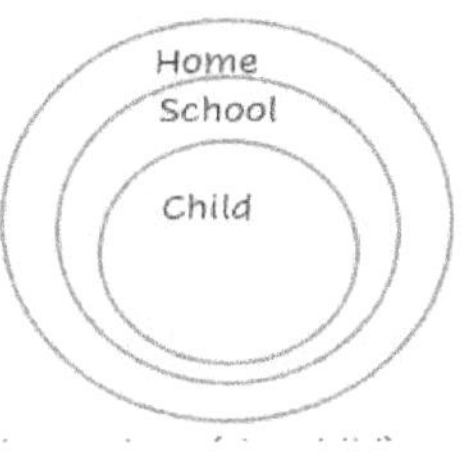

success and have had the good fortune of having parents who have trusted me with their children and supported my efforts. With this behind a teacher, any good idea you have becomes easy to implement, as you have the 'home' team to back you up. One cannot stress enough how important it is for the home and school to be in tandem. As shared in a previous entry, the home encompasses everything, including school, for the child. It surrounds them and becomes the outer shell of security for them.

For teachers, summer vacation is a time to recharge batteries, but come August, it is time to get the classroom ready for the children who will call that room theirs for the next 9 months. I happen to be one of those teachers who uses her summer vacation in much the same way.

So, one summer, I was making a new set of **Class Rules.** I was going to be in a new school and teaching a much younger age group than I currently did. So, these rules needed to be easy-to-read and understand. I am sure there is nothing worse for a child than being asked to read something and do it, but finding out it is completely 'Greek' to them! As a teacher, you want to avoid situations like this, especially in the first week when the primary focus is 'settling in' and getting to know one another. So, I decided to keep it simple. I came up with four things that I felt would suffice. My first draft looked like this:

DON'T TALK

PUT YOUR HAND UP

SIT PROPERLY

LISTEN CAREFULLY

Of course, that is not something I could display as it sounded too much like orders. So, I then began to think of things I would say to encourage the children... and then came the 'Eureka' moment for me! This is what I wrote... 'Do Your Best'. It is just one rule, but it permeates every single aspect of a child's behaviour, endeavours and interactions and becomes something of an aspiration. So that became **RULE No.1... the only rule...**

Do Your Best!

It became, and still is, the 'go-to' phrase in my classroom. "Is this your best ....?" It causes the child to reflect on their work, words, actions, etc. and then make the changes. It is funny that I have just one expectation in my classroom, but ... think about it. If you are expecting a child's best, then that is most likely what you will get. At the end of the day, that's what every teacher wants: for every child to experience that feeling of accomplishment and pride at something being done the best they could possibly do it.

How do our expectations affect children's psyches? How high do expectations need to be to enable children to reach their full potential? Should expectations be different for different children? What is an expectation? Anyone?

The Oxford dictionary describes expectations as 'a belief that something will happen because it is likely'. Are attributes like one's behaviour, nature and self-worth things that can show change because of expectations placed on an individual (in this case, a child)?

So, to come back to the question at the beginning of this entry … my expectations are high because they demand a certain amount of effort, but they are consistent with what the children expect from me, too. It goes both ways. All teachers are the same in this respect

… they want the best for the children in their classrooms. As a teacher and a parent, I know this to be true.

I remember a little girl, Nina, in my Grade 1 class one year. She was a victim of low expectations and no consequences at home. Her mum was the loveliest, most polite, well-mannered person, and yet Nina was her complete opposite in every way except one; Nina was highly intelligent, just like her mum. Her mum would chat with me every day, and one day, she mentioned that because of Nina's rudeness, the family was not welcome at her mother's home in the UK. Now, I never knew my grandparents, but my children did, and they are so much richer for it. The love, 'spoiling', cuddles and stories that come from our grandparents are invaluable. Nina was preventing herself from enjoying time with her 'Gran', and it was clear that neither she nor her mum were sure how to fix it. I wasn't sure either, but I knew one thing: love and consistency could fix any bumps that we come across. So that's what we did...we made sure Nina felt loved, and we created some non-negotiables for home and expectations that matched the ones at school. The circles were going to come through for us yet again! I told Mum that this would only work if she stayed completely firm on the non-negotiables and did it with lots of love, especially when Nina had tantrums and non-compliance.

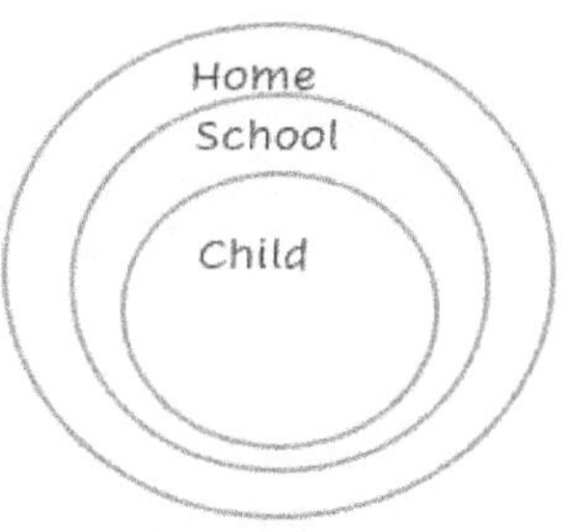

I also told Nina that her mum would keep me posted on her progress, so I was looking forward to hearing all about how 'grown up' she was at home, just like she was at school. Like all teachers, I was careful not to make Mum feel inadequate, and I promised to support her in any way I could.

The Christmas holidays arrived, and Nina and her family visited relatives, including Gran. When they came back, her mum was ecstatic! Gran had commented that this Nina, the one who minded her 'P's and Q's' (manners), was welcome in her home anytime. Woo hoo!! Wasn't that something? Nina saw firsthand the effect of her efforts, and she was so proud of herself. "I love my Gran, Miss, and now she says I can come visit whenever I like."

So, go ahead … set expectations for your children and help them accomplish their dreams. You are doing your child a HUGE disservice by making allowances for poor performance!

Keep your expectations high enough to aspire to but not so high that they become unattainable. Communicate these to your child's teacher so that you get the support you need and then give the support needed. It is full circles, entwined and encompassing ... providing security, confidence and inspiration.

-49-

Warm wishes and hugs,
Periwinkle

Dear Diary,

"My child is being bullied ... the school needs to do something." There is so much talk and awareness about bullying. We do so much to spread awareness, like an anti-bullying week, decorating a door, showing solidarity with this worldwide initiative, etc., etc...then please explain to me why this is not going away.

I would like to actually address this in two parts:

- **the bully**

- **the 'bullied' (no victims)**

I firmly believe that if we want our children not to be bullies, then we need to show them by example. My father was a school principal, and without raising his voice, he could be heard across an auditorium... without a microphone! He commanded respect and got it ... from students and staff! I had the good fortune of growing up with parents who believed in the saying below.

A good **EDUCATION** begins **@ HOME**... you cannot blame a school for not nurturing values in your child that you have not instilled first.

Take, for example, a little boy 'Tom', who is very creative, playful, etc. and decides to draw pictures on the wall in the living room with his crayons. Dad comes along (after a long, hard day at the office) and yells at him (with an expletive or two), snatches the crayon out of Tom's hand, pushes him away from the wall and sends him away. Now imagine this is dad's reaction to every 'naughty' (playful, fun) thing.

Over Time...Lessons Tom learned:

- Use a loud, angry voice

- Angry words are okay

- Push and shove; snatch too!

- Choose someone smaller (insignificant or younger, less important) than yourself.

One day, Tom is with his younger sibling, Daisy. They are both colouring at the table. She accidentally colours on one of his sheets. I'll give you one guess of how he is going to react!

The Bible clearly says, 'Train up a child in the way he should go, even when he is old he will not depart from it' - Proverbs 22:6

It's all in the instructions and your example.

It goes straight to my **#1 rule...Do Your Best!** Consistently high expectations ... for both teacher and student, in this case, parent and child.

Let's come back to our little example with Tom, Dad and Daisy... some questions...

- **What could Dad have done differently?**

- **What would the outcome have been?**

- **What would Tom's lessons look like?**

- **Why would this matter?**

Every BULLY **usually** has the following:

- A teacher/example/person to emulate

- A temper

- A lower self-esteem/overconfidence

- No expectations to aspire to

Everyone **'bullied'** usually has the following:

- Mild manners

- Smaller stature

- Different outlook

- Intelligence (most often)

These are, of course, generalisations. None of the above are bad things for anyone to have... they are just being used wrongly.

A bully is a bully only because he has been shown how, and the 'bullied' is bullied only because he has been shown how. Our job is to reverse the learning and be examples so that the impact is equally positive.

So, we tackle the 'bullied' first. We give him the strategies and tools needed to make him feel safe. I am talking about primary school children here, so naturally, if the children are older, then different methods are to be used. In this book, I have 'targeted' (for want of another word) primary/elementary school children and younger' therefore please do bear this in mind.

I think this 'strategies' thing needs a separate entry, so...hang on ...Let's say bye for now, only to meet again on another page... ***à bientôt***!

Warm wishes and hugs,
Periwinkle

Dear Diary,

And we are back!

What is **bullying?** It is when words and actions are hurting another person *repeatedly.*

In my mind, strategies are the that one needs to be tried in different ways before successfully opening a locked door to reveal the treasure that lies behind it. There is no such thing as a foolproof strategy, especially when dealing with children. That's why we may sometimes need to try many 'keys' before we have success.

Bullying can be experienced in many forms, and I have found in my experience that verbal bullying is one of the most difficult ones to identify and deal with. Words have such power, and from a young age, children need to be taught how to use them responsibly and with care; especially when there are feelings of resentment or anger at wrongful accusations and expressions of superiority.

Many schools have strategies like WITTS, etc.

W-walk away

I-ignore

TT-tell a teacher

S-seek help

This is good when it works and when children have confidence, self-esteem and friends. These are very helpful in stopping a bully from continuing inappropriate behaviour.

My worry has always been for the 'bullied' who do not have the above 'safety nets'. What happens then?

As a parent and a teacher, I have encountered this problem far too many times, which is why I question the awareness days so much.

Q. What tools do we need to sharpen as parents, teachers, carers, and adults?

Q. What are the tools we need to help our children sharpen?

As responsible adults with children in our care, we must first look inward. Are we the examples that our children should follow?

Transform the words you speak in your home to your loved ones if you truly want to see change. The Bible says that we are to be examples that guide our children ALL the time: talking to them at home, when we go out, even walking along... constantly teaching, listening to them and nurturing their minds as much as their bodies.

Both strategies outlined below are DIFFICULT!!!

STRATEGY 1:

From personal experience, the strategy I found that works very well is laughter. Don't smirk... it is true! Try it! When a bully says something mean... LAUGH! Laugh as if it is so funny, it cracks you up! Inside, you may be dying of humiliation, sadness, hate, anger...BUT outside, you laugh! Continue this for at least 2 weeks, and by week 3, the bully would have moved on as his/her tactics have not had the desired effect.

The thing with bullies is they feed off your fear, embarrassment, 'aloneness', need for acceptance, etc. When you laugh, you don't give them that feeling of power over you; it shows you don't care what they say or do. For a bully, that's the signal to move on to another target. You are not 'the bullied' anymore! This has worked well for my own children and is one of the simplest strategies that can be used on the spot, no matter what age group! It will get easier each day it is used...of course, you could help it along by telling your child to imagine the bully in a funny hat or with a pumpkin on their head...not so scary now, are they? Imagination is a SUPER- POWER... USE IT!!

This will work in middle school and high school, too. Of course, some people may think your child is weird for a bit, but that's okay. Weird is good! Nobody messes with weird!

STRATEGY 2:

Give your child a variety of 'alone time' games to use when they are not engaged in classwork (please inform the teacher, though). If there is an instance when a bully is not allowing your child to play or be part of a group activity, or excluding your child from a conversation, giving the 'brush off'...then this is something that will help support your child. Use the MAGIC 3

1. Tell your child every day how special and fantastic they are.

2. Explain that the bully is most likely not a very happy person and holds resentment; therefore, your child needs to be sensible and not get involved at that time.

3. Explain that the more your child yearns to be part of that group, the more the bully will enjoy excluding them...so don't even look in that direction. Play the 'alone time' games instead.

The truth is, don't let your child even go near them, don't ask to play, etc. Keep busy and show the bully how disinterested you are (even though you really want to be part of that group). Even if the bully tries to engage with your child, your child must not react. In fact, (and my own child did this) look right through the bully, like one can't see them. Don't show any emotion; don't show how much you want to be included by them. In this instance, ignorance truly is bliss!! Your child ignores and is soon left alone (bliss). It will have the desired effect...the bully will transfer their attention elsewhere. More importantly, though, it would have taught your child very important things about themselves: that they are...

- beautiful

- mature

- well-adjusted

They are ENOUGH!!

**Warm wishes and hugs,
Periwinkle**

Dear Diary,

"Ask your father." "Ask your mother..." Let's play ping-pong, shall we?

Well, in my experience, most parents resort to this more often than not when a child seeks permission so that...

1) ...it can be used to blame later

2) ...one can be 'off the hook'

3) ...one need not be accountable for a decision

All parents, including me, have resorted to this at some point in life, but when it becomes a habit where one parent makes <u>all</u> these decisions, it can be confusing for a child. Plus, it sends the message that only one parent has any 'power' in the equation, and therefore, only that parent is to be respected and obeyed.

A <u>united front</u> is not just a war strategy; it is the ONLY strategy that parents need to have, really. If they are together and have equal standing, chances are the children will view this and understand that both are in positions of power and have an equal say in the decisions for the family.

I remember a little boy from Southeast Asia who was in my class one year. He had been adopted as a baby by parents who were from two different continents. He knew that he was adopted, and his parents did not hide this fact, but even showed him the place where they had found him. I, for one, thought that was very brave of them. He had an Asian name and an English name...let's say Nathan.

On my class register, he was listed by his Asian name, so many parents and children who visited the class on the first day, the 'Get to Know' day, asked if Nathan was in my class. I said he wasn't, and the reaction every single time was sighs of relief and many "Oh, good!" or one very heartfelt "Thank goodness for you, Miss!"

I was puzzled. Who was this little person that nobody wanted to be around? What had this 5-6-year-old done that had such an impact? I had no idea at that time that Nathan was to be this little whirlwind...that nobody cared to befriend.

The lady who was the Head of Early Years had met me to 'prepare' me for this class I was being given... "because you are the only one who I think can handle this class" ...those were her exact words! I kid you not. She went through the list and would briefly stop and tell me a little 'background' for particular children. By background, I would need every ounce of patience, love, firmness and flexibility that I could muster if I wanted to get anywhere with them. I remember her telling me about Nathan and that I was getting him (his 'background' wasn't stellar, to say the least), so when I didn't see his name on my list, I will not lie; I was relieved. Anyway, I went to her with my list and the other Grade One class lists. I was the year Leader with ten sections of Grade 1, and Nathan's name was not on any list. I asked if he had been withdrawn, to which she shook her head and said, "That's Nathan's name," pointing to the Asian name on my class list. My heart sank; she saw my expression change because she asked me why my face fell. I told her how the parents and children who had visited my class had reacted when they found out he wasn't on my list. She nodded and said, "That's because Nathan has never had friends, just enemies."

My mind went into overdrive, and I began to plan all the ways in which I would make sure all the children made friends with him. I added another rule to <u>Do Your Best</u>: ' <u>Let's Be Friends</u>'. My teaching assistant, Lorna, had spoken to some of her friends who knew Nathan, and suffice it to say, the outlook was bleak. The stories we heard were not good, and Nathan seemed to be a child who could not be reached.

Anyway, to cut a long story short, Nathan arrived in Grade 1, and I placed him close to me at a set of four tables that had two girls and another Asian boy, hoping that at least that would make him feel comfortable, yet keep him restrained, having some girls around. Week 1 was fine, with everyone beginning to learn the routine and expectations of the class. We discussed our two class rules in-depth, and Nathan said nothing. He had a smirk on his face when he saw Rule 2. I watched him like a hawk. I documented everything I could think of and was relieved that so far, there had been no 'incidents' that colleagues had warned me about.

Of course, complacency is such an easy thing to slip into, and I was guilty of it because I did not proactively seek out strategies for Nathan, pre-empting behaviour issues....and then.. BANG! It happened...

The morning had just begun, and I was in the doorway of my classroom, greeting the children and the parents. Suddenly, we heard a loud shriek and screams and the sound of slapping! I moved quickly...leaving Lorna with the class. I speed-walked in the direction of the commotion, and lo and behold, it was Nathan! He was with his mother, a small, structured, meek lady; he had just slapped her and was yelling into her face, and she was doing her best to...apologise!!

I was furious! How on earth did this little, 2-foot-high human imagine this was acceptable behaviour? And what, may I ask, was the mother trying to do? I walked up to them and, with one quick movement, scooped Nathan away from her. I began to walk towards the school garden, and over my shoulder, I told her to drop off his stuff and go home. Leave! Nathan wriggled in my arms and tried to free his hands to lash out at me. Luckily, being stronger and bigger than him was to my advantage. I held on firmly, giving him just enough room to breathe and move but not to vent his anger with his fists.

At first, he only screamed for me to stop holding him (which I didn't do). I let him scream till he had no scream left. I kept hold of him the whole time. My shin was killing me...(oh yes! he had managed to get a kick to my shin when I picked him up).

My brain had a repertoire of choice phrases to say to him, but my heart said, 'sing to him'. I sang him the song that worked wonders with my own children, that put them to sleep every night... "Mama loves this little baby girl/boy" I substituted 'Mama' with 'Ms. Deirdre' and 'little' boy with 'Nathan' as I sang it over and over again to him, rocking him gently till he stopped screaming and his body began to relax. He listened to me singing for a while, and then he said to me, "I never heard this song." I didn't answer; I just waited to see if he had more to say...he did. "Nonebody sings for me." (he meant nobody)- "I like this song." I smiled and sang it over again. Then I asked why he had been so angry at his mum. He said Dad had travelled for work, and Mum had been told by Dad to 'let Nathan do anything' he wanted; Mum had obviously told Nathan to do something he didn't want to do, so he lashed out at her. His words being, "My dad says I only need to listen to him. What Mum says doesn't matter." I was shocked!

I was silent as I considered how to address this. The 'chat' with the parents was going to happen the minute dad got back! In the meantime, I was going to have to come up with something to affect Nathan in a positive way and send the message that this behaviour is not something I condone.

I remembered what a professor at training college had once said,

> *"Where will the kind, thoughtful, caring people come from for the next generation if our children are not taught the values of putting someone else's needs before their own?"*

This was a quote by Edith Schaffer that this professor would use often. Nathan was very aware of how his words made his mum feel. He could read her like a book! He knew it made her feel inadequate when he or his dad spoke down to her. I needed to make sure this came to a grinding halt.

I sent dad and mum a note to meet me and backed that up with an email as well to make sure it was received.

On the day of the 'chat', Nathan was the model child, and his behaviour was something to be witnessed! I called him out on it and asked how he had managed to be patient, tolerant and compliant the whole day. His reply is something I will never forget..." My dad says if I behave my best today, then he could easily make the ladies think everything was fine. I will get the toy/game/whatever I want." I was shocked beyond belief and made sure I wrote it down word for word. When I repeated this, suffice it to say Dad was not happy at being called out. I was firm but sympathetic; I explained that in parenting, there are no 'sides', no 'good cop bad cop', no '#1 parent and no non-authoritative parent'. BOTH parents have an equal standing and project a UNITED front, NO MATTER WHAT!

I asked him what he would like Nathan to be like as he grew and matured. His reply... "Let him be rich; money rules the world." So, I replied with the same quote shared above and asked if he would like his son to respond to his bribery or would he like Nathan's respect. I also requested this for his wife. He replied in the affirmative out of respect, so, I decided to work on that. If I could make life a little easier for Mum, Nathan and the other little tikes in my class, then I would do just that!

So, from then on, I began a home-school special connection that involved Mum giving me daily updates about home behaviour and me doing the same. I gave Nathan a WOW chart, where he had to give himself a ★ when he felt he had done something WOW. At first, there were WOWs everywhere, but then he had to explain and justify his choice and tell me why he thought these were WOW actions. Slowly, he began to learn the difference between WOW actions and expected actions.

When I go

Out of my

Way, actions.

Slowly but surely, the true Nathan began to emerge, and we all got to enjoy the company of a funny, active, cheerful team player who brought a smile to school every day. He also got a healthy dose of my 'magic hugs' to help him every day! We got to know a wonderful, unique, young man and are richer for it.

Nathan is now at university, how proud we all are of him!

'So many people go unnoticed and unappreciated because no one has ever taken the time with them to admire their uniqueness!!'

-John Powell

**Warm wishes and hugs,
Periwinkle**

Dear Diary,

"Miss, my child can't do without the tablet. At eating time, playtime, and now even bath time, it has to be in front of her. What do I do?"

The perennial dilemma for any adult, but for a teacher how to respond without hurting their feelings is really tricky. One does not want to make any parent feel inferior or less capable than the next person; at the same time, making sure that the advice given is specific and well received...without any bias, completely objective, professional.

When I began teaching, there was never any reason for this question since these were not popular devices yet. Fast-forward to the 21st century, and voila! The popularity of the tablet is phenomenal!

Let's face it: teachers are guilty of relying on these hand-held devices as much as the next person, and according to studies conducted by UNICEF, "Babies need humans, not screens"... so where does this leave busy adults with young children? Where does it leave anyone who cares for children? Where does it leave me? These questions drove me to think about what kind of educator I would be without the crutch of the 'device'. The answer was terrifying...." A slightly disorganised, fly-by-wire, fairly unprepared educator...that's who."

Don't get me wrong...these are wonderful inventions that have literally brought learning, fun and games, and entertainment into the hands of children; along with that, they have also brought some respite for parents and caregivers too.

A third thing it brought with it is overstimulation, a 24/7 buzz, zero social skills, an inability to read other humans' feelings and react to them appropriately, a need for constant 'alone' time, etc.

The parent who asked me this was genuinely perplexed and 'out of her depth' since the device had now become as much a crutch for her as it was for her child. I had to get to the bottom of the story, so I encouraged her to 'start at the beginning', so to speak. I asked pointed questions regarding screen time rules at home, how long ago did the tablet enter the child's life, who monitors what the child watches and how long she had been 'using' a hand-held device.

To my dismay, the parent disclosed that this little person had been introduced to the tablet when she was a mere 5 months old, as soon as she could sit up, basically. There were no screen time rules per se, just as and when the child needed to be quietened, entertained, 'bribed', and most of all, when the parent needed peace and quiet. Again, far be it from me to preach...I completely understand how busy a parent's life is. I am a mother of 3, and most days were downright exhausting! So, I am the first person to empathise with what this mum was going through. She had a super stressful job, as did her husband, and travelling was also an expectation for them both. That's how 21st-century parents roll...busy, busy, busy... run, run, run...worry, worry, worry... focus, focus, focus... we all know the drill. I applaud the parents of today; you are real superheroes! **But in all this, we cannot forget the little lives** that are inextricably entwined with ours. The lives that we need to nurture and guide the lives that matter too much to be anything less than diligently preserved... our tomorrows!

Through the book, I have spoken about **STREAM** rewards, the **5M's**, expectations and the one most important rule; I have also spoken about the importance of being an adult to the children in our care. We can be **different OR indifferent**...the choice is ours.

So, to get back to our mum in question, I reassured her that there was nothing I wouldn't do to support her or help her think of ways to help her little one along the way.

I had a sort of reputation at the school of having a very 'mum' outlook to my educating, and that came with a way of explaining things that no matter who you were, you got the picture really quick!

So, I started to outline, right from babyhood, how screen time was not always the most appropriate choice and how babies need human interaction to develop their communication skills since all communication is non-verbal at this stage of their growth. A two-way interaction between baby and adult is vital for brain development. As they grow and continue to have a screen in front of them, it becomes increasingly difficult for them to imagine and create games to play with other children, like Pirates, Prince and Princesses or Police and Robbers, etc. For a brain to develop, it needs stimuli from the outside world and time to process them. When someone is reading a story aloud, it allows the child to imagine and process the words, images, and sounds (voices) that cause brain activity and development.

"I am bored. What should I do?" Boredom is very important for children to experience so that they can deal with it and come up with ways to deal with it on their own. When I am asked this question, I put it back on the child with my own question. "Is there an activity in the classroom you can do independently?" I know full well that I have dozens of extra things for the children to do once they have finished their 'Must Do' task. So, there can never be a 'lull' moment for them. So, this was something I suggested to this parent to give her child some other alternatives that she would be able to succeed at on her own. We all know that the absorption of onscreen images and print affects children's attention span and focus. Non-screen activities are ideal for encouraging your child away from their device.

Indoor games vs. indoor games

- Jenga   screen/device games
- Lego
- Board Games
  (Ludo, Chess, Scrabble, Monopoly etc.)
- Jigsaw Puzzles
- Fishing games

Of course, these are just suggestions, as I told her, and ideally her little one should be given an opportunity to run around outside (weather permitting) with her friends/siblings every day.

Reading faces and having social skills are two factors that help develop empathy. A screen keeps them devoid of this very important human need to be able to put oneself into another's shoes.

Another thing I suggested that seemed to shock her more than it did me was, **"Learn to say NO and teach her child to understand the meaning of the word NO."**

<u>"I can't do that, I want to give her everything I did not have as a child myself, Miss."</u> I gave her the example of my own son, when he was very young, about 2 or 3 years of age, on days that we would go to the store or the supermarket

together we would have the same conversation before we left the house.

Me: I have ...... much money for the groceries, and we are not buying anything for ourselves today.

Son: Ok.

Me: When we get to the shops, I will not be getting anything other than the groceries, so no sweets or toys for us. *(never you always us- the rule was for us both).

Son: Okay.

When we would get to the shops more often than not there would be an instant where he would tug on my hand and ask for something. Then I would have to remind him, very gently but with a firm 'No', that we had discussed this at home and decided we would not be getting anything other than groceries. Of course, there would be days when the conversation would be amended slightly to include one treat for us to buy at the shops.

I explained that it was not a terrible thing to say 'No' sometimes. I proceeded to remind her why she had come to talk to me in the first place. With a gentle smile and a hug, I told her that she could still do that and also instil in her child an appreciation for all the wonderful things and experiences that both her loving parents were giving her.

"How?"

Together, we mapped out what we wanted to accomplish for this child. Mum and Dad would

be a united front and would encourage their little one to be part of their 'team'. We came up with a few important tips:

1. One rule at a time

Mum/Dad would begin with monitoring screen time, limiting it to a few times in the day after certain things were completed e.g. After schoolwork is done, after bathing not during. We still allowed it at the table as weening off anything requires patience and love, gradually removing the 'need' for the object.

2. Give options

Instead of the tablet, Mum/Dad would let the child choose two alternative non-screen activities she could do by herself or with a person of her choosing (provided the person was available too).

3. **Be prepared** for pushback- hug and stay firm.

Mum/Dad was to prepare a star chart so the child could collect stars for **not** complaining, **not** throwing tantrums or any behaviour that would be the opposite of the 'Do Your Best' rule from school that was to be implemented at home as well.

It was expected that the child would sometimes be non-compliant, so lots of hugs and positive words were to be used, but Mum and Dad would not give in. Just like the saying 'united we stand, divided we fall', Mum and Dad would stand together and 'sing from the same song sheet', so to speak.

4. Reward

Every success was to be rewarded with a star; every wobbly success was also to be rewarded with words of praise. Mum and Dad would be sure to use my standard "back pocket" words of affirmation to encourage the behaviour that they wanted. Home and school working together - concentric circles of support.

5. Celebrate

Mum and Dad were to celebrate how wonderful and 'grown up' their little one was, and between them, they had to come up with a treat that they would, as a team, be able to share together.

I am overjoyed to report that after a few initial hiccups and a few wobbly steps, things began to settle, and our beautiful little girl began to evolve and her schoolwork began to show such promise and improvement that I had to call the parents in to show my appreciation and express how wonderful it was to see the positive change in their child. All because they took the time to ask and act together to truly nurture their little blossom.

I love it when things work, don't you?

It's the best feeling in the world!

**Warm wishes and hugs,
Periwinkle**

Dear Diary,

"Miss, I can't think of any ideas for my story."

Another statement that used to really irk me till I realised that it really was a problem for the children! They really were finding it difficult to use their own thoughts and their own imagination. It dawned on me that this was another side effect of the proverbial 'tablet' and screen dependency the children had developed over the years; I included myself in the percentage of time children are on their devices. Of course, I am not saying that using a device to further learning or for some fun is bad...in fact, it is a good thing to be technologically sound, especially today. Technology is everywhere in everything, even a fridge! So, no, that is not at all what I am saying here. My view is that when this same device becomes a crutch, and one cannot do anything without it, then there is a red flag waving wildly, begging for you to notice it.

As parents, teachers, and child-carers, the easiest thing to do when you want to keep children occupied, is to say,

"Go play on your device" OR "Go onto ......app and play .... game." Again, it's not a bad idea either for us or the child/children, but when this becomes the norm and not the exception, then again, out comes the red flag!

In my class, as in most classrooms, teachers expect children to be full of ideas and stories that they want to tell. It is a bit disappointing to find that over the last few years, this is not the case, and as a teacher, there is nothing scarier for me than a loss of imagination in a child. Where will all the future inventions come from if we don't expose them to their imagination? I began to think about things that would help, simple things that don't cost anything but have wonderful results.

We had started our topic on Space in Science, so I got my daughter to write a note on my board pretending to be an alien from 'Planet Zog', and I made her ask a question that would need an answer from the class. As they walked in that day, they looked at the board and then began whispering about it. I pretended not to see the message, so I started to tell them about the day and their schedule, etc., as was my usual practice. Then one of them raised their hand and said, "Miss, there is a message on the board. Didn't you see it?" Of course, I shook my head and said I hadn't seen it; I asked who wrote it, etc. There was a buzz in the classroom, and the children were excited to talk about it. I was thrilled that my little idea had had the desired effect! My children were chatting about who this was, where they came from, why they chose our class, etc., etc., so then I announced that we were going to write a reply to this friendly alien and answer the question (s) it had asked us. That got a favourable response from the class, so I taught them how to write an informal letter (which was the English writing genre we were doing that week).

Lesson 1: We discussed how to address an informal letter and how to start and finish such a letter.

Lesson 2: We wrote down all our 'suggestions', theirs and mine, and we wrote out a whole class reply for the alien.

Then we carried on with our day, and at the end of the day, one of the children asked me if this was really an 'alien'. I am not one to lie, but, neither will I miss an opportunity to suggest a 'maybe'. So, I replied that I wasn't sure, but because we had such fun writing today, I hoped it would happen more often. That seemed to satisfy, and I was relieved that I didn't have to go into details of Planet Zog!

The next day, there was another note, the third day again, and so it continued for the duration of our topic on Space. We managed to get through a variety of genres in writing thanks to the 'alien' from Planet Zog. Based on what the 'alien' would ask, I was able to get them to imagine the weather on Planet Zog (setting of a fiction story), what our class 'alien' looked like and what it liked and disliked (character study/ development) and some things that happened to the 'alien' (plot) and how things were solved (solution/ending).

The children in my class shared this exciting mystery with the children in other classes, and soon, 'alien notes' began appearing in other classes, too! My daughter was thrilled to be a part of the whole thing, and the children would tell her what the 'alien' had written when she came to my room at the end of each day. Suffice it to say, that was one of the ways I got a little imagination to rear its beautiful head in my classroom. Of course, there are umpteen ideas and things one does to get results like this, and I would say, please use things like this to show your children the wonderful world of their imagination... of course, be sure to enjoy it yourself.

At home, too, maybe a helpful little person visits your home and leaves notes for the children.... let your imagination run away with you for a bit. It truly is worth investing time in...nothing like a bit of magic to brighten up your day!

**Warm wishes and hugs,
Periwinkle**

Dear Diary,

"Miss, my child has spent …. years in school and still cannot …. I don't know how he will manage."

Hanz's mum was worried and quite distressed about the fact that her son was not at the same level as the other children in my year 3 class. She was right to some extent; Hanz should have been able to get some of his sounds and letters, etc., in the years he had spent at school. Then I remembered that we had just come out of COVID and that the children had been doing online work for the past 18 months (in some cases more than that). So, I did what any teacher would do: I reassured her that things would settle and that I would do my best to help Hanz catch up and close the gaps a bit. Of course, I did not promise miracles, but I did promise all the support he would need to succeed. Then I asked for a promise from her as well. She raised an eyebrow, questioning my request. I told her that she would need to set aside time every day, including weekends, to sit and listen to Hanz and work with him if needed. She happily agreed and so began our journey with Hanz and his mum. Pretty soon, we could both see the difference in him. Because he had begun to read simple words, his confidence grew, he participated more, and we celebrated every little success with great '*Dhoom Dhaam*' as they say in India, meaning a lot of loud celebration. The year ended, and Hanz could read at the level of the class because of two very important things: belief in himself and support from his immediate environment (home and school). The circle diagram does work, people!

I had the pleasure of bumping into him a few months ago at the mall. I heard my name yelled loudly across the corridor and the thumping of feet behind me. As I turned around, this tall ball of energy ran into me and hugged me around the waist. It was Hanz, with his mum, hurrying along behind him with a gentleman I had never seen before. They were smiling, and once the greetings were done, I found out that the gentleman was Hanz's dad, whom I had not met before due to his busy work schedule and travel commitments. It was wonderful to finally meet him, and then I was given the biggest gift of all... Hanz said to his dad, "This is the teacher who took the time to teach me to read." I had tears in my eyes, and so did his parents. Then his dad shared that he was in year 5 and that reading was 'easy peasy' for him now. Of course, I was quick to credit Mum, too, as it would have taken so much longer to see results if it hadn't been for her. Then she shook her head and said..."But you gave us the tools and language rules to work with." Step by Step, everything falls into place!

Speaking of tools and rules, there was this little girl in my Grade 2 class one year, in the early days of my teaching career, who came from one of the most prominent business families in the city. They lived in a penthouse at the very top of one of the tallest buildings at that time. She was a delightful little girl with a quirky personality, and her giggle was one of the most infectious ever! However, for all her quirks, smiles, and giggles, she had one very large area of motor skills that was never allowed to develop: managing to walk up and down a flight of stairs. She would come to school by car, and her nanny would carry her up the stairs to my classroom on the first floor. I had never seen this before in my life, so on Day 2 of school, I told the nanny there would be no carrying the child up or down the stairs. The nanny was horrified and told me that she was not allowed to do so and that she would be in trouble. "We always use the lift(elevator); we never take her up the stairs.

She doesn't know how to go down or up the stairs." I could not believe it. How was this possible? I did not want any trouble, so I called home and requested permission to teach this little lady how to use the stairs. The parents were very respectful, as they are in India, toward all teachers, and gave me the green light. So began the Saga of the Stairs, as we began to call it. I soon realised that this little girl had no concept of depth, so going downstairs would result in her losing her balance and falling head-first on the staircase. She had no concept of fear either and was willing to try anything to teach herself to climb and descend stairs on her own. I began her 'training' by holding her hand and taking one step at a time with both feet; she held my hand and the side rail, going up and down the stairs. Then, she progressed to going up the stairs with a partner and down with me. Once she could do that without help, we graduated to doing this with one foot on each stair. My reward was a huge smile and a warm hug each time she managed something she previously thought was too difficult. By the end of the third month of school, our quirky little girl was manoeuvring the stairs like a pro! By month 6, she was running up and down the stairs, and we had to start restraining her! Her parents couldn't believe it, but the nanny took the cake when she said..." Now, I will need a leash, as she will be all over the place!" We all laughed loudly; Geet included; she thought it was ever so funny!

What was it that Einstein said? *"One who fears failure limits his activities."*

All it takes is tiny baby steps...the rest, as they say, is history.

Warm wishes and hugs,
Periwinkle

Dear Diary,

When I first started teaching, terms like ADHD, ASD, ADD, etc., were unheard of. Gradually, we were introduced to these different terms, which gave us an idea of how some children were different from others in that they learned differently and had different needs, too. For us teachers, things had to change quickly... 'differentiation' was the new buzzword, as were 'levels of ability' and catering to 'needs of the class', etc. It was exhilarating for me to learn and apply these things in my classroom, as I am sure with most teachers; at last, we were being trained to support every child in our classrooms. It was a very exciting time for me, and in such a time, I was introduced to a wonderful set of children in my year 1 class, one of whom was Ned. His parents were a lovely couple, but they were very reluctant to share much about their son at first. So, I had to start my learning journey with Ned as we sailed along a fairly choppy sea, learning with and from each other. I soon realised Ned was definitely different from any child I had come across, and he had a few quirks that I had no clue how to deal with. For example, he only used the colour orange (his mum would only send packs of orange colouring pencils to school for him). I found this extremely odd and said so to one of the other teachers in our Achievement Centre (SEN department). She then told me that little Ned had Asperger's, which was high-functioning autism. So that's why Ned was brilliant at reading, numeracy, photography, and video making, way above the level of the rest of the class. Ned refused to write; he deigned to colour sometimes, and even then, only orange. I spoke to his parents and said that I would like to try teaching him to use a pencil to write sentences and eventually stories, to which they both replied in the affirmative, but they warned me that they had tried and failed miserably because Ned got very upset and started 'flapping'. I knew what they meant because I had witnessed a few such episodes myself. At first, the flapping had taken me by surprise, but then, as time passed, I knew it was just a coping mechanism for Ned, and it didn't surprise me or the other children anymore.

Ned was such a smart cookie; he knew what I was trying to coax him to do, and he resisted with all his might and refused to use a regular HB pencil to write with. Then, one day, I decided to change tactics like any good commander would do, and I asked the whole class to choose their favourite colour pencil to write with for the day. They were asked to write why they chose this colour and how it makes them feel. Ned was shocked! I repeated my task to write a few sentences with their favourite colour pencil that day. We would use the same pencil for all subjects for that day. Everyone settled down to their writing task, including our friend Ned. I was so excited! I walked around the room and soon saw that Ned's work was outstanding in content, but sadly, the formation was lacking. I praised his effort and then asked if he found writing difficult. He nodded and replied that it took too long to write out his thoughts, which is why he didn't like writing. "Ned, what if I told you there was an easier way to form your letters to make writing faster? Would you be willing to try?" I asked. He looked at me as if I was asking him the dumbest question ever... "Duh!" he said with a cheeky grin. I introduced Ned to joined writing and how to let letters flow together. My years in training college learning the Marion Richardson, Sheila Strover, Cursive scripts, etc., all held me in good stead. Together, (he and I) came up with something that worked for him. That was Step 1... Step 2 would take much more time since it required Ned to use an HB pencil to write with. Since my favourite colour writing day had worked so well, I came up with another idea: Miss D's favourite pencil writing day; of course, you guessed it, my favourite pencil was the humble HB, my trustworthy writing tool of choice. I purchased some really cool pencils for this and gave each child a pencil of their choice from my 'favourite pencil box'. I instructed them to use 'my' pencils the whole day and return them at the end of the day. So, it was their responsibility to sharpen it, keep it carefully, and make sure it was returned in the same state that it was given (slightly shorter, of course). The pride a little child gets in being given something of value from their teacher knows no bounds. I had 21 of the most careful, responsible mini-Me's that day. It was so amusing and yet so humbling because of how much they cared about my pencils. Ned also worked hard that day using the pencil, using his own script, and finding out how much he was capable of if he just put his mind to it. Gradually, I saw Ned evolve into this risk-taker who tried things previously thought to be not worth the effort and succeed at it, too! Oh, joy!

The feeling that one gets when all your efforts have not been in vain, is one of the most fulfilling ever!

My heart was full...thank you, Ned, for having a go!

That's all anyone can ask or hope for.

**Warm wishes and hugs,
Periwinkle**

Dear Diary,

Speaking of having a go brings to mind a few other recipients of my 'have a go' tactics... if one can call it that. It's something that both teachers and parents alike can easily accomplish when they are like-minded towards a particular goal. In this case, the goal was to develop self-confidence and the ability to try something even though one may not be totally comfortable with it. It's like my relationship with roller coasters; I find them exhilarating.... to watch, not actually experience! In the same way, some children are watchers, not doers, and those are the ones I like to 'have a go' at. I will put them in situations where they must rely on their abilities to succeed. As many adults do, I too am prone to making up my mind about the children in my class, something like putting them in a box and then making them remain there, 'coz that's what they can do or that's as much as they can do. You know the thing about such boxes: the lids can be blown off at anytime. I learned this very early in my career, so when I am faced with children who are already in boxes, I try to be the one helping to blow the lids off! I remember having a little boy, Dan, and a little girl, Frieda. Both were in their little boxes, timid, shy, and unwilling to put themselves out there much. Very often, we, as adults, subdue our children purely out of the need to not see them get hurt or shunned or do as well as another child in sports, etc.

Dan and Frieda were actually in my class but in different schools. Dan was from the UK, and Frieda was from Asia.

Both children were bright and capable, popular with their classmates, responsible, polite and well-behaved. The type of children any teacher would want in their classroom. I cherished them immensely till I noticed that there was also something I needed to help them with, something that I knew would help them step out into their future without apprehension, something that their parents would also want very much and would be able to help me with... their self-confidence. Both children were very eloquent when speaking to small groups of their peers and gradually with me too, but whole class discussions, debates, elocution, etc., were things that large audience situations seemed to be a stumbling block for them both. I was careful not to be impatient as I knew how capable they were, but they didn't know that for themselves.

That was the mountain we needed to help them climb- home and school, the mountain of self-doubt.

I spoke to the parents and as all of us parents know, when a teacher addresses a need in your child, you will do everything it takes to reach out and help. This was exactly what these parents did, too; they were ever willing and ready to get their children 'out of their shell' and into the spotlight...or at least somewhere near it. This is where I need to separate both children, as the tactics we used were different for each of them.

Operation DAN:

Dan had a wonderful group of friends at school, so I would make sure that he had just a word or two to say whenever his group had to present something to the class. I always placed him in the same group so that he became very comfortable with them and slowly started sharing his thoughts and ideas within the group, without any prompting from the assistant teacher or me. I positioned myself in close proximity to his group but did not invade his safe place in order for him to feel independent and adequate. His mum thought of asking him to record his thoughts about his day, what he learned, etc., on his device, then play it back to her. She then began sending them to me, and so I mentioned this to him and said I was so proud of how well he spoke. One day, Dan was confident enough to let me share one of his recordings with the class, but me, being the prodder that I am, played some of the recording and then pretended that it had stopped working on its own. I suggested he tell us the last bit of it. He nodded and began to speak to the whole class with his clear voice. In the end, all of us clapped loudly for him, and he blushed profusely and sat down. I could see the change in him, and soon quiet little Dan became not-so-quiet little Dan, and we were introduced to this eloquent little human with so much to say and share. Well done, mum! It took both hands to clap, and clap we did!!!

Operation FRIEDA:

Frieda was tall for her age and the rest of her classmates were much shorter, so this meant that she usually stood at the end of our line.

She was a model student with excellent spelling, reading and writing scores. Math was a breeze, as was Science and other subjects. The only areas she seemed to struggle with were oral work, presenting, debating, and reciting by herself and even within a group. She would not put herself forward, even though I knew she could easily accomplish something like this. This continued for a while, and ideas began to form in my mind of how I was going to encourage this talented little girl to show everyone her true self, the self that she kept hidden, which I had seen glimpses of when she animatedly spoke about something she had done or seen, to her close friends. That's when I saw her eyes light up and her face flush with excitement as she related the event with clarity and in great detail.

One day, I had a 'EUREKA' moment. I knew exactly how Sir Isaac Newton must have felt when the apple fell from the tree, allowing him to come up with his theory about gravity.

We were due to present an assembly in a month, so I was busy preparing the script for the children and organising things for this. I still remember that we decided to write the story of

Farmer Duck and use that story to drive the moral at the end of the assembly. I assigned roles to different students but not to Frieda. I asked her if she would like to help me train everyone instead. She reluctantly agreed after I assured her that I would be there the whole time. Together, she and I worked as a team; I made her practice each child's lines with the child who was saying them and watched as she gave them ideas on how to say their lines. It was amazing to watch (of course, on the quiet), and I didn't let on that I knew what she was doing. Each time we practised, I would praise the child, saying their lines, and then one of them had the presence of mind to pipe up that Frieda had provided feedback and suggestions on how the lines could be said better. I said how fantastic that was and how good she was at saying these lines.

Then I gave her a piece of paper, the narrator's lines that I had not assigned to anyone yet. I asked her to read it and let me know how she thought they should be said. I asked her to practice and say them for me the next day. Unknown to her, I had already told her dad I would do this and asked him to help her if needed. I gave him the idea of using a mirror for her to practice with so she could 'see' herself as she spoke.

The next day, Frieda came to school and burst into the classroom, eyes shining and cheeks flushed, grinning from ear to ear. We were all taken aback as Frieda was not known to give in to such expressive behaviour. "Miss, I said the lines out loud. Then, my dad recorded my voice and made me listen to it; I sounded so good. I am so proud of myself." We asked her to say the lines for us, and she did; she had learned them by heart, full of confidence. We clapped and cheered for her, and then I told her that she was our narrator for the assembly. She didn't shy away in fear but instead stood up to her full height and said, " I can do it, Miss." And she did! She was the best narrator I could ask for.

Many years later, I met her dad, and he was so happy to see me. He brought me up to speed on Frieda's progress and said she was heading the Junior School debate team at her new school. Then I reminded him how he and I had brought our talented little Frieda out from the back of the line to the very front of it.

If there is any takeaway from this anecdote, it is this...Don't think about what world you are building for your children; think about what children you are building for the world.

Warm wishes and hugs,
Periwinkle

Dear Diary,

It was the same year I met Dan and Ned, and I had the pleasure of meeting little Starr. Her father worked for a very well-known software giant while Mum was a stay-at home mum. Starr was tiny and reminded me of a little elf with her blond hair that fell in waves around her little face. She had a cute button nose and a pair of sparkly, green eyes that shone with mischief and fun.

I learned that she had very poor muscle tone in her abdominal muscles, which meant she could sit up for long lengths of time, she would suddenly just flop over. So her mum had brought in a special cushion for her to use that helped with posture and allowed Starr to remain seated for longer. I made sure that she and I developed a signal when she couldn't sit anymore and needed to move around or lie down. This worked really well till... I soon found that Starr was a lot like her name; she did everything a star would do, including choosing things she would and would not do. She began using the signals whenever there was a task that she preferred not to do.

Fortunately, or unfortunately, I am the kind of person who documents everything, and soon, a pattern began to take shape. There seemed to be a direct link between more formal/written tasks and her inability to sit in her seat. As I am sure you have gathered thus far, I am certainly not the type of person to back down from a challenge or who will ignore outright misuse of a privilege. At the same time, I needed to make sure she would be alright and that any decision I took would not be detrimental to her progress and overall experiences at school. This is something that any parent would do, too, with their child's best interests at heart; sometimes, one needs to be 'cruel to be kind'. One needs to make tough calls in order to guide your child correctly in the long run.

Starr also hated to wear shoes and chose to go barefoot throughout the building. She needed to feel the floor so her brain could send signals to her body to walk or run, etc. This was something that troubled the head of the school as she didn't want 'children running about with no shoes on' at such a prestigious school. It was my job to make sure Starr wore shoes and sat in a chair so she could go to year 2. I failed to see how this was even a requirement, but...I had to try.

Anyway, to get back to the 'pattern' that was developing, I knew I had to nip it in the bud or else it could grow into something uncontrollable. So, the first thing I did was to reorganise my timetable and place all the 'heavy' lessons at the start of the day when everyone was fresh and their brains were bright and awake. I also decided that Starr would be in charge of tidying up books after each lesson, which would give her a sense of purpose and the opportunity to move around before she used the signal. I told Mum to try the same thing at home, to give Starr a sense of purpose and not to do everything for her, just like we did at school. So, school expectations carried over to the home as well, and the transition for Starr was seamless and helped her move her mind from school mode to home mode more easily. Slowly, she realised that she could do more before she had to use the signal, giving her a sense of ownership of her learning and her own ability. She began to push herself and set her own goals, which was amazing to watch.

What happened to the shoe thing, you ask? Well, I will tell you, we cheated a little on that one... I asked her mum to stitch Starr a pair of cloth shoes with a thin silicon sole that allowed her to 'feel' the floor without having to remove the shoes at all. For the outside times, Starr was allowed to wear her rubber sandals as a special concession by the head after we explained why Starr needed them. All in all, the shoe issue was solved with a little quick thinking on our part and oodles of understanding from our headteacher, too.

I once heard this quote that has stuck with me for ages. *"At any given moment we have but two choices; to step into growth or step back into safety."*

Fortunately for us, Starr chose to grow and shine as bright as her name.

Warm wishes and hugs,
Periwinkle

Dear Diary,

Through the many years I have been teaching, I have interacted with many parents, and very often, the children say or do things that give a peek into their home life. This is when the lines of being a mother and being a teacher can merge. I became a teacher-mum, and my responses began to reflect this. Most teachers who like to truly teach have this trait... the teacher-mum syndrome! This is not restricted to the children alone. It is used equally with parents, too. I remember an incident that reassured me that teacher-mums are still as relevant today as they were years before.

There was this little boy in my class, let's call him 'Rafe', who was very sporty and bright. He stood taller than his classmates and was popular owing to his friendly, outgoing disposition. Throughout the year, he flourished in his school work and on the sports field as well.

It was after the winter holidays that I began to notice very subtle changes in his attitude and overall demeanour. He was less willing to abide by school rules and took to being rough with his classmates who were not as sporty as he was, which was not at all his nature thus far. His rapport with me hadn't changed per se, and he was still respectful and polite to all his teachers and adults at school. But I began to see a shift in his interactions with his classmates.

Then, one day, a child came to me in tears with a complaint about his good friend Rafe. From what I gleaned, Rafe had used a piece of playdough, fashioned into a shape and held it to his trousers and said, 'suck this'. I was horrified but outwardly did my best to remain calm. This was not the Rafe I knew, and it was not going to be easy, I thought, to get him to 'confess' to this incident. I went through all my go-to phrases, and then something my dad always said to me popped into my head. He always said, "The best time for the truth, no matter how unpleasant, is now."

So, I set tasks for my class while I asked for Rafe to 'help' me with an errand. As we walked to the photocopying room together, I asked him about what had happened with his friend in the bathroom that day. I asked if he had done what had been described, and at first, he looked surprised that I knew. I did not say I was told or who had spilt the beans; I merely asked if this had happened. I was careful not to sound accusatory and made sure he understood that I wanted to know his version of what happened.

I did, however, say that I would appreciate the truth, so it would be a good idea for him to just be honest and explain what happened.

He admitted to doing it and saying the words to which my next question was how did he get to learn something like this. He then told me that his friends at home, who he played basketball with, spoke to each other like that in fun. "Miss, it was just a joke, and I didn't mean it seriously," he said. I nodded and hugged him with my 'magic hug' and reminded him that things like that can be easily misunderstood, so it was a good idea not to repeat such stuff. He said he would apologise to his friend, which I thought was very mature, and I said as much to him. He swelled with pride and then said, "It will be my best sorry ever, Miss!"

When his mum came to school to pick him up that afternoon, I asked if she had a few minutes to spare. Being the lovely lady she was, she immediately told her two boys, Rafe and Ryan, to go to the school canteen while she chatted with me. I explained what had transpired, and she turned all kinds of shades of red with embarrassment. I made sure that I only gave her the very basic outline of the incident at school but focused on who Rafe played with once he got home. We chatted for a bit, and she realised that Rafe had made friends with a group of sporty teenagers who loved basketball and had invited Rafe to play with them every afternoon during the holidays. He had continued to play with them on the weekends once school began, and obviously, he had been privy to some language and actions that were not appropriate for a child his age. She was mortified that she hadn't checked on him while he was with them and said she would be more careful from then on.

The takeaway from this whole debacle is that she could not stop thanking me for spotting the changes in him, even though they were ever so subtle, and then talking to her about it. She said these words, and they still cause me to tear up. "Miss, I can't tell you what it means to me to know that you care about my Rafe so much. I don't have any family here, and today, I feel as if I have someone from my family who I can talk to, who will understand and not judge. You are not just a teacher to my Rafe; you are his family, too." Teacher-mum syndrome is here to stay!!

It just takes a few mistimed, misguided statements to impact a child ...(in her words... he was seven, not 17!)

In fact, I remember another incident where I had to have 'the chat' with a parent about the ideas and concepts that were being presented to a child who was becoming the parent's friend instead of being their child...the operative word being **child**.

The parent in question was a really lovely, with the most charming disposition and extremely caring to those around her. She, however, seemed to think her son had grown up and was now able to function as a teenager at age 7. This little boy, let's say 'Jack', was the sweetest child ever and emulated the characteristics of his mum to the T. He was polite, friendly, caring and, most of all, completely aware of how to make and keep friendships. This trait endeared him to everyone in the class, including children and adults. He really was the sweetest thing, except when he suddenly began to demonstrate slightly over-enthusiastic caring, especially towards certain girl classmates. He would bring them gifts like roses, chocolate, 'love' notes, etc. At first, they enjoyed the attention, but slowly, they began to start pushing him away. I watched in fascination and then sorrow as this beautiful little boy began to experience being shunned for no other reason than his classmates did not understand him and his actions. They were a bit too mature for them to grasp, as it was something a teenager would do rather than a 7-year-old.

I remember as if it were yesterday, I asked to meet Mum after school on a day when he had his after school activity session. She was most enthusiastic and welcomed the chance to sit and talk about her 'big boy'. At first, we chatted about his schoolwork and his attitude, etc., and then I asked if all was well at home. Her face changed, and I saw utter defeat and helplessness written all over it. Moisture pricked her eyes as she told me things weren't going very well. She and her husband had just gotten divorced at the start of the school year, and she was still adjusting, as was our little Jack.

I just listened to my heart, as anyone in my place would have, and held her hands in mine as she spoke about what Jack was adjusting to, life without 'dad' being at home, so he had to be the 'grown up boy' instead. She spelt out how she had recently started dating again and told Jack all about her dates and the presents she was getting, etc. She revealed that Jack asked her why she was given gifts like roses and chocolates from people. She answered that her girlfriends got gifts like these from their boyfriends. Then she asked Jack who his girlfriend was, and he had mentioned all the girls in his class. She said she was very proud that he was so popular with the girls, and she had pushed him to give them presents and write love notes.

I was at a loss for words, (which doesn't happen very often may I remind you) how could a perfectly sane and lovely adult think it was okay to push her little boy to 'grow up' so soon?

I probed further and found out that many of mum's friends also did the same with their children. So, there was a plethora of these ' grown-ups' in her friend circle, and this was the norm, not the exception. How was I to get through to her that her advice was actually harming her child's social interactions at school?

Time was not on my side that day, so I scheduled a follow-up time for us to reassess how we could help Jack.

The week passed, and on that Friday, Jack came to me and said, "Miss, I don't want to be a big boy. I want to be a kid again." My heart broke for this young man who was trying to be everything his mum wanted and knew that he wasn't ready for that yet. I held him close and told him he had my love and support- at school, he could be whoever he wanted to be, the best that he could be without a care in the world. He grinned at me and went off to play.

On Monday, his mum met me and asked for a few minutes. Normally, I do not appreciate talking with parents at this time as it is the time when the class is preparing for the day, and we are setting expectations and going over our schedule, etc. However, I made an exception because of the emotions I saw on her face. We sat outside, and she apologised to me. It seems that Jack had told her about his conversation with me and my reply. He said," Miss Deirdre said I can be whoever I want to be and be the best I can be, so why is that not enough for you, too? I am 7, not 17!" I was shocked that this little human had such wisdom and maturity! I was also grateful that his mum had allowed him the space to express his feelings, which is so very important. She then said," I realised that I was putting my baggage on my son, who could not carry it. Thank you for being his safe place, Miss."

Most true teachers, educators, etc., would do the same. To be an educator with purpose, one must put oneself close enough to the fire, and with a simple Shloka and lighting an oil lamp every evening. The woman of the house (mother) should do it and set an example for her daughters.

5. Join the armed forces if your family has a history of serving the nation or if you are inclined towards it.

6. Always support the vulnerable.

7. Donate to temples and poor Hindus liberally.

8. Be proud and courageous of your Dharma.

9. Support in the modern education of all poor Hindus so they have a good life.

10. Celebrate all Hindu festivals and make your children enjoy them and know the history and relevance of the festivals. Put your phones away during the Puja!

11. Perform last rites, monthly Amavasya and annual ceremonies of your parents and ancestors as per the Sastras with the help of a learned Pundit.

12. Put pressure on the Governments to free our temples so they can be managed by the community that it belongs to. This is a constitutional right that all our governments so far have gone against. ONLY HINDU TEMPLES ARE UNDER GOVERNMENT CONTROL UNCONSTITUTIONALLY- Religious institutions of other religions are not under Government control. (If temples have been

freed from Government control by the time you read this book, congratulations- please make sure it stays this way as funds donated by Hindus should be used for the upliftment of the Hindu society and Dharmic purposes. The Government has other sources from taxes for other general welfare schemes for all citizens.)

13. Do Annaadhanam (Feed the poor free of cost) regularly.

14. Visit your Kula Deivam (Hereditary family deity) temple at least once a year and make sure the temple is in good shape.

15. Make being Dharmic the new cool. Don't be woke - it makes you live a lie and harms your inner self. Sanatana Dharma is the most inclusive you can get so wear it on your sleeve proudly. If you don't respect yourself, you can never truly respect another.

CHAPTER 27

WHAT IS THE ROLE OF A VAISYA IN THE MODERN WORLD?

Whether we like it or not, right or wrong, today we are all Vaishyas. But if you belong to the hereditary Vaishya Varna, understand that there should always be Dharma and ethics in business. Today we are seeing the mushrooming of several companies that make money only for the founders and lose money for others. As a dharmic businessman or businesswoman one must always do our 100% to ensure fairness to all stakeholders. Being profitable and also contributing to dharmic causes. Historically the Vaishyas were extremely important pillars for the support of all other Varnas as they would donate liberally to all those who had other duties/vocations. So as a Vaishya in the modern world you should work hard and also donate liberally for Dharmic causes.

Action Points for Vaishyas:

1. **Donate to Veda Patashalas regularly**
2. **Support all Poor Hindus.**

3. Perform the thread ceremony for your sons and make sure the father and son do the Sandhyavandhanam and Gayatri Mantra thrice a day. Make your children learn the Vedas and recite them.

4. Teach your daughters simple pujas that they can do daily like offering food to God, birds with a simple Shloka and lighting an oil lamp every evening. The woman of the house (mother) should do it and set an example for her daughters.

5. Take a keen interest and support temple Khumbabishekams (Ritual and mantras to rejuvenate the deity done every 12 years) and reconstruction of old temples.

6. Support in the modern education of all poor Hindus so they have a good life,

7. Earn and share your wealth for dharmic causes.

8. Celebrate all Hindu festivals and make them an enjoyable family affair for your children. Make your children enjoy them and know the history and relevance of the festivals. Keep away your phones during the Puja!

9. DO NOT SPEAK ILL OF YOUR RELIGION EVER. STAY UNITED

10. Perform last rites, monthly Amavasya and annual ceremonies of your parents and ancestors as per the Sastras with the help of a learned Pundit.

11. Support in the modern education of all poor Hindus so they have a good life.

12. Put pressure on the Governments to free our temples so they can be managed by the community that it belongs to. This is a constitutional right that all our governments so far have gone against. ONLY HINDU TEMPLES ARE UNDER GOVERNMENT CONTROL UNCONSTITUTIONALLY- Religious institutions of other religions are not under Government control. (If temples have been freed from Government control by the time you read this book, congratulations- please make sure it stays this way as funds donated by Hindus should be used for the upliftment of the Hindu society and Dharmic purposes. The Government has other sources from taxes for other general welfare schemes for all citizens.)

13. Do Annaadhanam regularly.

14. Visit your Kula Deivam temple at least once a year and make sure the temple is in good shape.

15. Make being Dharmic the new cool. Don't be woke - it makes you live a lie and harms your inner self. Sanatana Dharma is the most inclusive you can get so wear it on your sleeve proudly. If you don't respect yourself, you can never truly respect another.

CHAPTER 28

WHAT IS THE ROLE OF OTHER CASTES IN THE MODERN WORLD?

Firstly, as a Brahmin, I fold my hands and ask for heartfelt forgiveness if any of my ancestors treated people belonging to the Shudra Varna as inferior to them. Please accept my heartfelt apology as those who felt they were superior to any human being were absolutely wrong as per Sanatana Dharma (Many of them also got carried away by the Britishers' devious plan by thinking they were superior. But we cannot blame the British for everything as we should have upheld our Dharma by experiencing it, studying it and knowing from the heart that all human beings and all creatures are but physical manifestations of the same Paramatma). All the other castes and sub-castes today referred to as backward castes have been the pillars of our society. Could our society function without their selfless service and labour for the sustenance and betterment of society? Could all the amazing temples have been built without their hard work and labour?

No way! Can a factory function today without the blue collar worker? Similarly even when the Varna system was in force, nothing would have functioned without the selfless service to society of the Shudras. Please understand Lord Krishna belonged to the Yadava community (Supposedly a backward caste/OBC as per today's crude caste system used by politicians). Do we not revere him? What does this say? The knowledgeable realize that self-realization and God realization have no caste! Mahaperiyava also points out that the Shudras have an advantage and are not bound by rituals that other Varnas are duty-bound to perform, and they (Shudras) can become inwardly pure through Karma Yoga or Nishkama Karma (i.e. doing one's duty in the material world without hankering after rewards or returns as Lord Krishna explains in the Bhagavad Gita).

Many would be surprised to know that we had many great Shudra kings who were great warriors and upheld Dharma proudly:

1. The **Nanda dynasty** of the imperial **Magadha** (5th and 4th century BCE)
2. The **Kushan dynasty** (Kanishka and others) in Northwest India (1st to 4th century CE)
3. The Kings ruling over **Sindh and Matipur** (7th century CE)
4. King **Lokanatha** mentioned in the Tippera inscription (8th century CE) 5. King **Pala dynasty of Bengal** (8th to 12th century CE)
5. King **Divvoka** of North Bengal (11th century CE)

6. The **Kakatiya dynasty of Telangana** (12th to 14th century CE)

7. King **Viracoda** mentioned in the Pithapuram inscription (12th century CE) 9. The **Reddi dynasty** of Kondavidu Reddi kingdom was established in southern India by Prolaya Vema Reddi (14th - 15th century CE)

8. The **Nayak dynasty** mentioned in the Akkalpundi grant

9. King **Vanduvaraja**/ Palalvaraja/ Thiruvaranga of Draksarana inscription

10. The **Chola** dynasty

11. The **Pandya** dynasty

There would have been many more and the above is just a sample I could find when I did my research,

After writing this chapter, I was planning a short weekend break with my family to some place in India. My wife suggested Chatrapati Shambaji Nagar (Aurangabad) as there was direct flight connectivity and the weather was less hot than other places in June. I jumped at the idea as I wanted to see the Ajanta and Ellora caves* and show the historic relevance of Shivaji Maharaj to my kids and visit the Greeshneshwar temple (one of the 12 Jyotir Lingas). I had never heard of the Daulatabad fort, but God's way of taking us to places that matter is amazing. We landed up at Daulatabad fort and I was amazed! A little about this fort and why it is relevant to this chapter and our understanding of Sanatana Dharma...

Daulatabad Fort originally Deogiri Fort, is a historic fortified citadel located in Daulatabad village near Chatrapati Sambhaji Nagar (Aurangabad) Maharashtra, India. It was the capital of the Yadavas (9th century – 14th century CE), for a brief time the capital of the Delhi Sultanate (1327–1334), and later a secondary capital of the Ahmadnagar Sultanate (1499–1636). The Yadavas were Shudras, supposedly a backward caste. But for those who understand Sanatana Dharma at its core - All are equal despite their differences in the physical world as the Paramatma is in all of us irrespective of our caste, creed, sex, orientation or religion. The Yadavas in my intuitive opinion could possibly be the direct descendants of Lord Krishna as he was a Yadava too. Do we not worship him as the all-knowing Supreme being, did anyone irrespective of their caste discount him? Bharat had many Yadava and various sects of Shudra kings like the Cholas. Lord Rama Was a Kshatriya and a supreme upholder of Dharma. The Daulatabad fort where I went with my family is one of the world's most impenetrable forts built by the Yadavas (Led by Monarch Billama V) who were great warriors, leaders strategists and upholders of Dharma! The Mughals (Allaudin Khilji's Army) could penetrate only through deceit by stopping all supplies of food and water into the fort. It is a must visit and amazing to visit with kids. Let us stay united, people. We can be united only if we understand the absolute oneness of all of us by understanding the Karmakanda (rituals) and finally the jnanakanda (vedantic philosophy of meditative knowing of Supreme bliss the formless omnipresent, omniscient Paramatma) of our Vedas, Shastras and Sanatana Dharma. A few photos I took at this amazing fort:

So, In the modern world too, you people can be anything and do anything you can visualize and dream of. While I have no political affiliations whatsoever, as I type this, our Honourable Prime Minister Mr. Narendra Modi who is now recognized as one of the strongest leaders geopolitically comes from the OBC caste, our Honourable President Smt Droupadi Murmu comes from the

Schedule Tribe Caste. Both these individuals have seen several hardships in their life but are today serving 140 crore Indians in the top leadership positions, to make our country scale great heights. I feel these are two modern day examples of what people from other castes can do if they set their heart and mind to it, with God's grace of course. Today we have some of the best ISRO scientists, world class doctors, engineers, entrepreneurs, leaders and people of all fields who belong to other castes and sub-castes.

So I would urge all of you to rise up and dream big as Dr. Abdul Kalam said, and drop all inferiority complexes please. You are no more or no less than people of any other caste, creed or religion. Move from being a victim to a master of your own destiny. If you are able to dream, study and work hard the sky is the limit for you. **While doing whatever you want to in a Dharmic manner in the material world, please keep up and help in maintaining your village temples and keep up your culture, customs and family rituals. Please support people who are economically backward from your community and from all Hindu communities if you are in a position to do so. Please talk to the most vulnerable and support them so they don't get coerced or forced into converting to another religion.**

CHAPTER 29

IS EATING NON VEGETARIAN FOOD BAD OR GOOD?

There is no moralistic good or bad in Sanatana Dharma. Everything was scientific. It is silly to take a moralistic view point and brand non vegetarians bad and vegetarians as good. Food habits and accepted foods in Sanatana Dharma depended on the community's vocation. Kshatriyas and Shudras could eat meat because of the physically challenging jobs they had while Brahmins and Vaishyas were predominantly vegetarian because their vocations were sedentary. In the ancient times our Rishis ate meat, but over time they experimented the impact of food on their physiology and psychology and stopped eating meat. The Brahmin is supposed to study and chant the Vedas and dedicate his life to self-realization and for the good of the world, he slowly realized that food that is rajasic activates desires and anger which go against his quest to meditate for the well-being of the world. The Brahmin must keep his energies as pure as possible and it starts with what he puts into his body and the degree of harm it has inflicted on another sentient being. Food is classified into Sattvik, Rajasik and Tammasik as per Ayurveda, and it is advisable for those in the spiritual path to avoid Rajasik and Tamasik foods. Basically for anyone in the spiritual path controlling ones senses is very important, and for that, eating food that is sattvik is very important. All food that we eat, whether vegetarian or non-vegetarian harms another living being. The idea is to move to foods that harm the least when we are on a spiritual quest. Jains for example don't eat any root vegetables as that kills the plant itself. I personally stopped eating onion and garlic around 10 years ago for spiritual reasons and could see a huge difference in my physiology and ability to meditate. So, we have to stop any moralistic discussions on food and understand it scientifically, which is what Sanatana Dharma has always done. Even many non-vegetarian Hindus abstain from eating meat on auspicious days and this is a method of gaining control over our senses so we are not compulsive in anything we do.

Summing up, the food that we eat should enhance our lives, not impact our earth adversely, and aid our spiritual progress. If we can, let us tread the path of least harm in our food choices is what I would say, with no judgement to anybody's food habits or preferences.

CHAPTER 30

THE IMPORTANCE OF CEREMONIES FOR THE DEPARTED

Throughout this book we have spoken a lot about the importance of the sounds of the Vedas and yajnas that are for the celestials/deities who in turn bless us with prosperity in the physical world and beyond. Now before reading this chapter, please go back to **Chapter12: Do Astral and Subtle Planes Exist** and reread it. In that chapter it was made clear that our relatives who have passed away exist in the Astral/subtle planes that are called Pitru lokas. So now let us understand the extremely important duties of Hindus to perform not only the last rights when a person's father or mother passes away, but also do the Amavasya tarpanam every month and the Shrardham (Shradh) annually for our deceased father or mother which also includes 7 generations of our ancestors in the mantras. Now since we know the astral planes exist, if we do not offer pinda and arghya to our ancestors do we not do them and ourselves grave injustice? So the rites for the celestials (deities) we must perform with devotion while the rites for our pitrus (departed ancestors) we must perform with faith as per Mahaperiyava. We have to take care of our mother and father (I add mother in-law and father-in-law for both man and woman) when they are alive and make sure they are comfortable in their old age. This is the least we can do for their sacrifices when we were young. So, Mahaperiyava says, after they depart it is our duty to do the Shraddha and offer libations. We offer sesame, water, balls of rice (pinda) and other food items in addition to doing homa in the fire. While we may think this is a mere ritual and the food offered remains in the physical world, like a money order sent from one place to another reaches without the money not being sent physically, the deities and celestials take what we offer to the departed souls to them. So what if the person is reborn? The amazing part is that no matter where the soul is reborn, the soul will not suffer for food and water if we do the requistite rites for the departed, according to Mahaperiyava. My understanding is that the fire makes gross to subtle and also it is the karmic bond, Shraddha (faith) and thought take our offerings in the physical world to the souls for whom we do the rites. We should not think that we are greater than the celestials and departed. As per Sanatana Dharma we in the physical world and the celestials and departed in the astral world share a symbiotic relationship. While we do our duty (Karmas) they bless us with prosperity in return.

So how come other religions don't have these rites and rituals? Do their ancestors suffer? Do they suffer?

No, even in our religion Sanyasis who are spiritually mature and directly in realization of the Paramatma do not have to perform these rites for their parents. In other religions too they do not have any concept of celestials and deities so they do not have these rituals as they worship the One God directly. Because of this are these rituals just baseless? Not at all, if we are born as a Hindu we are bound by these rituals and have to perform them for the well-being of our family and future generations. A lot of things we may not be able to explain scientifically yet (or may never be able to), but if our rishis and Jagadhgurus have told us of their importance, it is wise to follow them. So are we polytheistic while other religions like Islam, Christianity, Buddhism etc. are monotheistic? Again the answer is no. We adopt a scientific path from karma yoga, Samskaras to sannyasa in a step by step manner to the same One God. So we move from the dualistic Vedas, rituals etc. to Vedanta and the Advaita philosophy of non-duality and oneness.

CHAPTER 31

WHAT IS NISHKAMA KARMA? KARMA YOGA

Nishkama Karma simply put means doing one's duty without desire for benefits or results. This is one of the most important teachings of Lord Krishna in the Bhagavad Gita. Karma Yoga (Nishkama Karma) is something that all of us have to train our minds to do to lead a happy, peaceful life while slowly achieving inner purity. Have I achieved that state? No chance! I still have too many desires and wants. I wouldn't be writing this very book if I didn't feel a sense of dissatisfaction with status quo. However I have removed any monetary reward from the sales of this book and will be donating all my Author Earnings after tax to dharmic causes. So my desire is for a unified Hindu community and a unified peaceful world free of hatred. In my business and in our jobs we all have wants and desires, but it is important for us to slowly but surely do what is needed and focus on the process and not worry about the result. Nishkama Karma is the core value system of my organization Bril (You can find it here on our website: https://brilindia. com/about-me) and every new recruit is taught this philosophy and made to apply it to the best of his / her ability. What Karma Yoga does is that it slowly brings a sense of acceptance that we really do not control the results. What is under our control are only our actions. While it is a beautiful philosophy, it is extremely hard to practice it because with our limited knowledge we always hope and pray for the results of our actions the way we want it. Sometimes, God has other plans and trust me, his plan is the best plan. Even if results are not materially rewarding and something appears to be a failure, there would be a life lesson and something that possibly impacts your spiritual life positively. The more we practice Nishkama Karma the more we become inwardly pure by reducing our desires and slowly but surely preventing the cycle of birth and death. The more our desires, we will keep coming back to fulfill those endless desires is what Sanatana Dharma says.

CHAPTER 32

WE ARE ALL UNTOUCHABLES

While this is a controversial subject, this has to be addressed as a lot of people bash Hinduism saying we practice untouchability. Are you wondering if I have gone mad when I say we are all untouchable? No. I mean it. My grandmother would not touch anyone after she bathed and till she cooked and finished her daily Puja. Was she being mean and rude? No. She knew the importance of a pure body and its positive impact on the mind when she cooks and offers the food to God first by way of a Puja (We must always thank the Lord for the food he gives us despite us having so many flaws in us). I cannot go to Kanchipuram and hug my Guru Bala Periyava, though I have great love for him and I know he loves me dearly as he loves everyone unconditionally. Is he treating me badly? Not at all! He needs to keep himself pure so he can bless us and undertake strict austerities so he can do his penance and the Chandramouleswarar Puja as ordained by Bhagavad Pada Adi Shankara for all our well-being. We must understand the importance of hygiene and personal space given in Sanatana Dharma. The Brahmins especially had to keep their bodies extremely clean and pure to undertake the rigorous demands of rituals and rites and chanting of the Vedas which we have seen are subjects of thought, sound and energy. For example, can the Chef in any big hotel's kitchen that takes hygiene seriously exchange clothes with the AC mechanic who has soiled clothes by virtue of his vocation, before cooking? Does this make the Chef a superior person to the AC mechanic in the same hotel? While all are equal, Sanatana Dharma understood that our bodies are a collection of vasanas (Impressions) based on our past birth and current vocations and food habits. Nobody, I repeat, Nobody is inferior or superior and of course some people ill-treated people of other Varnas and continue to do so because of their sheer ignorance. Now why do I say we are all untouchables? Do you remember Covid? What happened then? Why did we have to wear a mask and stay away from people? Why did we stop hugging each other? In Hinduism our rishis and Gurus always knew that while the body is our personal temple, it is intrinsically not clean. The body sweats, it has blood, saliva, urine and faeces in it all the time. We knew that to minimize the chance of infection and from a personal hygiene stand point it is best to avoid physical contact as far as possible except with our closest relations like parents, spouse and children – hence I say we are all untouchables irrespective of our caste, creed, sex, orientation, religion etc. Beyond this, there is something called Runanabandha which is the physical memory that each of our bodies carry from blood relations and sexual contact. So from the slightest touch to intimate relations the degrees of Runanbandha we accumulate varies from minimal to maximum. Sadhguru (HH Jaggi Vasudev) explains this concept well and I am taking excerpts from his blog:

Runanubandha, is a certain kind of physical memory. You pick up runanubandha in many ways, but sexual relationships have maximum impact in terms of the amount of memory that they leave, compared to any other kind of touch, or any substance you come in touch with.

This is not a question of guilt or ridding yourself of guilt. This is not about social conditioning – we are only looking at the existential aspects of life. The body has its own memory. Today, there is research happening in this direction. To put it in a simplified way, let us say for example, your father, when he was a child, liked to play with round objects, round pebbles, and things like that, and he developed a certain level of involvement with them. As his child, without knowing why, you will tend to choose similar things. It is proven that these repetitions happen. This is simply because you carry a certain genetic material.

Runanabandha in Men and Women:

Runanubandha is the physical memory that you carry within you. This memory can be acquired due to blood relationships or sexual relationships. When it comes to sexual relationships, a woman's body has much more memory. When it comes to genetic material, a man's body has much more memory. Generally, over eighteen to twenty-one years of age, a woman's body carries less physical memory than a man's body. The main reason why nature has done this is because a woman has to bear a child from a man who is not genetically connected with her. For her to carry the child to term, it is very important that her genetic memory is less.

Many women can vouch for this – the moment you get pregnant, without knowing why, your emotions for your parents and other blood relatives will fade to some extent. At least in India, when you are pregnant, you go back to your mother to seek her support, for practical reasons. But the emotional connection will decrease dramatically. This is part of nature's system to enable a mother to comfortably accommodate the genetic material of the child's father within her system. Otherwise, if the mother's body has too much memory of her own parentage, the unborn child, which carries different genetic material, will struggle.

Runanubandha cannot be equated with the genetic factors that are being transmitted from parent to child. It is a physical memory of where you came from – not necessarily in terms of colour of your skin, shape of your nose, how you are built, and so on. It is just that even if you as much as hold someone's hand, you develop runanubandha. This is why in India, people greet you with folded hands. They do not want to acquire runanubandha. The same applies for passing on certain substances, like salt, sesame seeds, or soil – people never take them from somebody else's hands, to avoid developing runanubandha. Since this culture is essentially oriented towards liberation, this awareness and these sensitivities are there not to build bondage in life, but to keep it only to the extent that is absolutely necessary.

The body remembers any kind of intimacy – not only with another physical body, but with any physical substance. Certain types of substances have more of an impact than others. You will see, if a yogi comes to sit somewhere, he will walk up and down, look here and there, feel different places, and then settle down in a particular place. Because they are sensitive to what is suitable for their system.

You will only be conscious about these things if you are working in a certain way with your system. Otherwise, if every day you are eating all kinds of things that you have no control about; if you are travelling a lot, you cannot maintain all this. But generally, for long periods of time, people did not move anywhere. Even just two generations ago, most people would be born, live, and die in the same house. Today, you come in touch with many more people and substances, and it has become all-the-more relevant to be conscious of not developing too much runanubandha.

CHAPTER 33

VEDANTA

Today a lot of Hindus say rituals are useless and that they are Vedantins. While the Vedas themselves talk about the highest order being Vedanta and non-duality . i.e. knowing the oneness of Paramatma (Universal Consciousness / God) and Jivatma (Individual consciousness), we must ask ourselves if we are spiritually mature to go straight to Vedanta by discounting the other steps. So, are the Karmakaanda (ritualistic side of vedas) and Jnaanakaanda (Philosophic and Vedantic side of Vedas) in contradiction to one another? While the Karmakandas enjoins us to worship various deities and celestials and lays down rules for the same, the Jnanakanda constituted by the Upanishads ridicules the worshiper of deities as a dim-witted person no better than a beast. While it appears strange that the latter part of the Vedas contradicts the former part of it, we should realize that spiritual maturity is a process. Are we all mature enough to overcome our senses and gunas and realize God directly? Is it right to do this without performing the rituals to please the celestials and gain worldly prosperity and happiness? However, as we mature spiritually only, can we slowly move away to purely meditation and realize the Paramatma within. I can emphatically say most of us are not inwardly pure and do not have the depth of spiritual experience to bypass the steps and become a Vedantin straight away. Speaking for myself, I am not equipoised, I get angry, I have fear of death and attached to the body though I intellectually know this body is but perishable while my Aatman is indestructible, I still have desires that are worldly – do I have the right to discount all rituals that will help me slowly eliminate my flaws and realize my true self? The Gayatri Mantra is the mantra of mantras that has the meaning of three Vedas namely Rig Veda, Yajur Veda and Sama Veda in it, is it not important for me to chant it every day for myself and the wellbeing of all people and creatures? Can a LKG kid like me go straight to Engineering or do an MBA or PHD? Does he/she not have to take it step by step? The beauty of Sanatana Dharma is that it is as much for a spiritual novice as it is for a Sanyasi and a mature all-knowing God realized soul. Our saints, rishis and Gurus are evidence for this. Because the rituals and samskaras purify us and slowly take us towards aatmajnyana. For many of us this could take us several births to achieve, and we must not only meditate as per Vedanta, but we must also perform all our rituals and rites as per the Dharma Sastras to slowly but surely achieve a state of oneness with the Paramatma in this birth or in the coming births.

CHAPTER 34

AHIMSA OR SITUATIONAL LEADERSHIP

Today terrorists are killing Hindus and people of other religions in Jammu and Kashmir's bordering areas. Can we sit and say our Army has to practice only Ahimsa and not defend us by neutralizing the terrorists? While Ahimsa and love for all is the ultimate goal, the beauty of Sanatana Dharma is situational leadership and the Army's Dharma is to fight and protect our land from adharmic forces. As Lord Krishna says, do what is needed to be done without hatred or attachment and with God in your heart. Easier said than done when Hindus are killed just for their faith, but we must act unitedly and make sure our civilization survives the onslaught of Adharmic forces. So, the beauty of our religion is that it has greats like Chanakya who elaborate the nuances of tough love and leadership. While we must understand the oneness of us all, we cannot allow adharma to happen and stay silent, as the we too become accomplices to this adharma. Our Kshatriyas were masters at warfare but dharmic even in war. We Hindus have become meek and have let down Hindus of Pakistan and Bangladesh because we have been fooled into believing that only Ahimsa is Hinduism. Today Hindus are down from 27% to 1.9% in Pakistan and down from 30% to 7% in Bangladesh if we compare the 1947 and 2023 population. While these are in different countries today, we are making the same mistake in Jammu and Kashmir where regularly Hindus are being killed just for being Hindus. We should be ashamed as a people that we have let down our Kashmiri Pundits (3 lakh of them) who are still scared to go back to Kashmir where their homes are. What can we do, we are helpless you may say. We may not be equipped to go to the battlefield and fight alongside the Army, but can we not use our collective might to make the world take notice? Are we so dead that we can't even post about it on social media collectively to make the world understand that religious persecution of Hindus is not tolerated in the modern civilized world? We Hindus believe that somebody will save Hinduism and Hindus, but sadly we have forgotten the importance of speaking the truth and supporting Dharma and condemning adharma because we are scared that people will call us bigots. Understand dear Hindus, if you understand Sanatana Dharma at its core, you cannot hate anyone or any religion, but if you forget Lord Krishna's words to Arjuna when he got scared to fight his brothers and elders, we will cease to exist in the generations to come. The force of the Kali Yuga a period of 432000 years will get harder and harder for future generations if we Hindus only care to earn a living, have a good spouse, have a house or multiple houses and a few cars. We have to think beyond this mundane existence in supporting Dharma. If you lose a few friends for speaking up for Hindu causes and speaking up against terrorism against Hindus in specific and against any civilians at large, understand that they were never your true friends, and it is ok. It may appear tough initially but understand that speaking the truth in your heart sets you free! So, in a nutshell, Ahimsa and Love for all knowing we are all one is the absolute ultimate objective of Sanatana Dharma as the same Paramatma resides in all creatures, however situational leadership is equally important and it can be as simple as speaking up instead of staying silent for someone else to speak on your behalf. Imagine the impact of 1 billion of us speaking up against Adharma and speaking for Dharma on social media? Now not even .01% of Hindus speak up when Hindus are killed just for their faith or about the Kashmiri Pundit or for the protection of our children and women. Outrage always seems to be super selective and only when it is the popular 'politically correct' voice. If we speak together even Governments will stand up and take note, else it will become par for the course and civilizational degradation is unavoidable. **Speaking the truth without hating any religion or community is the most important aspect. Do not brandish all people of any religion or community as bad but speak up when there is religious persecution of Hindus and religious persecution of people of any religion (Do**

not parrot only the popular voice- look beyond and support Dharma at all times). United we stand, divided we will surely fall as those who do not learn from history are condemned to repeat it. Let us not forget that Lord Ram fought against Ravana not only for his beloved wife Sita, but also to protect Dharma! Let us not forget Lord Krishna's very clear message to Arjuna during the war in the Bhagavad Gita.

Similarly, while we all want our temples freed from Government control which we are entitled to as per Article 26 of our constitution, how many of us are actually speaking up aloud regularly about this matter? All Governments since independence are dipping into temple funds meant only for Dharmic purposes and using it wantonly. I am talking about a constitutional right that Mahaperiyava was instrumental in drafting now being used for all other religions except Hindus! We should be ashamed of ourselves if we cannot raise a voice collectively and get our temples freed from Government control. It is not easy because all Governments want to dip into the nearly Rs. 50000 crores collected annually from our temples!

CHAPTER 35

OH HINDUS WAKE UP FROM YOUR SLUMBER, FIND THAT SPARK AND MAKE IT A FIRE!

Oh, my dear Hindus, please I beg you to wake up from your slumber and find that spark in you and unite as Hindus in Bharath and around the world. Please throw away all your differences of caste and language and be united as one, as this is a matter of civilizational and existential threat towards our great religion, which is the world's oldest and most inclusive religion. We were fighting amongst ourselves and were made to suffer 1000s of years of invasions. Millions of people have died during these invasions and for a free Bharath we live in today. It is our duty to safeguard our Dharma for the sake of not only our religion but for the safety of ALL religions of the world. Bharath has so many religions flourishing ONLY because Hindus are in majority. We belong to the most inclusive religion in the world, but the forces of adharma that want to destroy Dharma are huge. Bharath is a democracy, and democracies are at the mercy of demography. If the demography of undemocratic ideologies increases, we will not have a democracy at all anymore. Worse, if divisive ideologies are allowed to grow, our country may not exist in its current form and may split into pieces as has happened in the past. Bharath extended up to Afghanistan, but today we have even lost a portion of Kashmir and are still fighting to get it back. The diversity of this great land can truly exist ONLY if we the Hindus are in majority. Do not worry if you are called communal for stating this uncomfortable truth because data and statistics don't lie and if wanting the same laws for every citizen of our country to ensure demographic balance to retain the diversity of this great land is communal, wear it on your sleeve as a badge of honour. Our Kashmiri Pundit brothers and sisters still cannot go back to their homes in Kashmir. My Guru asks them to go bravely, but it is very hard to live in a hostile environment. See the population of Hindus in Pakistan and Bangladesh today. From 26% in 1947 Hindus today contribute to less than 2% today in Pakistan. Not only Hindus but the Christians have been reduced to 1.2% , Ahmedia Muslims have been reduced to 0.02% and the Sikhs are practically extinct in Pakistan and Bangladesh. So, am I saying Muslims are bad? Not at all, but the truth is we should aim for unity in diversity and not uniformity. This unity in diversity is the beauty of the world and it is up to us Hindus to fight to protect not only Hindus but the right of every individual on planet earth to practice their religion or faith without having to convert by force or coercion because all religions are TRUE and lead to the ONE TRUE GOD and we know that in our hearts and we must educate people so we end religious wars and eventually achieve world peace and peaceful coexistence of ALL people of all faiths!

Oh Hindus in Bharath and around the world, I call upon all of you to see the beauty of our religion and its 100% inclusive nature. If there is even a spark left in you, I call upon you to make that a fire and rise from your slumber for the sake of Dharma! Protecting dharma is difficult, nobody said it was easy. Lord Rama struggled through his life to protect it. His life was full of struggle, and he never shied away from taking the difficult path for the sake of Dharma and larger good of society and his Kingdom. Please dear Hindus of all Varnas, castes and subcastes, do not allow politicians or ANYONE to divide you on caste or linguistic lines. This will make us weak and fragile to hostile forces. Please be a Hindu first and fight for your Dharma, as nobody in the whole world will fight for us when we are in trouble. This is a civilizational battle, a battle of narrative, a battle against extremism and terrorism, a battle of good against evil, for the peace and coexistence of all religions in Bharath and an attempt to achieve world peace through Dharma is a constant. As Swami Vivekananda said, "Arise, Awake and Stop not till your goal is achieved."

So being a warrior to protect Dharma in your own way in the Kaliyugam sometimes can feel lonely but rest assured that Dharma Protects the one who protects it. So, rise above from your mundane life and work towards a larger cause – a brighter, safer, dharmic Bharath and a Vasudeiva Kutumbakkam (World is one family) for our future generations. **Be unapologetically Hindu!**

CHAPTER 36

BHAGAVATPADA ADI SHANKARACHARYA

This book and my efforts would be incomplete without a chapter on His Holiness Bhagavatpada Jagadguru Adi

Shankara. Adi Shankara is revered to be an Avatar of Lord Shiva, as without him we might not have Bharath in its current form. He was a unifier of all schools of thought of Sanatana Dharma. According to the Kanchi math, one of the 5 Mutts established by Adi Shankara himself, Adi Shankara was born in 509 BCE to a pious Nambudri Brahmin Family in Kalady (parents: Shivaguru and Aryamba) and attained siddhi in 477 BCE according to Kanchi Mahaperiyava (I will never dispute the wisdom and timelines given by Mahaperiyava as he was an embodiment of Ishwara himself). His maternal home where he was born is in a village called Velliyanadu in Kerala around 1.5 hours from Kochi airport and is managed by Chinmaya mission (The vibrations in the room he was born in are to be experienced to believe). In his short life of 32 years, he expounded the importance of Vedas and the Advaitha philosophy, unifying all schools of thought and even all religions! He walked the length and breadth of this country and established 5 Mutts **- Badrikashram Jyotirpeeth in the north, Dwarka's Shardha Peeth in the west, Govardhan Peetha in Puri in the east, and Sringeri Sharada Peetham in Chikkamagalur district, Karnataka and finally settled down in Kancheepuram.** Sri Adi Sankara, after his various tours through most parts of India, settled down at Kanchi to spend his final years. He caused to remodel the city and reconstruct the three principal temples -Sri Kamakshi, Sri Ekamranatha and Sri Varadaraja. **At Kanchi he established a Math for himself and founded a line of successors after him on the Peetha.** At present the presiding Shankaracharya is Pujyasree Sankara Vijayendra Saraswati Swamigal, the 70th Shankaracharya (Bala

Periyava). The 68th Shankaracharya of Kanchi Mutt was the great Jagadguru Chandrashekarendra Saraswati Swamigal fondly known as Maheperiyava and believed to be the reincarnation of Adi Shankara himself by many devotees. The 69th Shankaracharya was HH Jayendra Saraswati Swamigal. I feel blessed to have had darshan of all these three Gurus and continue to live in the shadow and benign grace of Bala Periyava now.

Adi Shankara lost his father at an early age. He made great strides in his education in his early years. When he was 8, he went to bathe in a river with his mother where a crocodile caught him. Adi Shankara told his mother that he would live only if she permitted him to become a Sanyasi. The mother out of love for her son's life agreed but on the condition that he would perform her last rites (Sanyasis have to severe ties with parents and renounce the world). So, Adi Shankara gave her his word. He started out in quest of a competent teacher, and eventually found Govinda Bhagavatpada (the disciple of Gaudapada) on the banks of the Narmada. He stayed with his Guru for a while. Under his command, he went to Kashi and Badri.

(Side Note: When he was in the Himalayas in his 20s, he intuitively knew that his mother was going to pass away. He kept his word and walked back to Kerala and was there for her when she passed away and performed her last rites as he had promised.)

It was during this period while in Badri when he was of twelve years of age, he wrote his most profound commentaries on the Vedanta Sutras of Badarayana, the principal Upanishads and the Bhagavad Gita which are known as Prasthanatraya, being the authorities on the Vedanta Sastras. The Bhashyas (commentaries) of Shankara are monumental works covering the import of the Vedic teachings and supplemented by clear reasoning and lucid exposition. This doctrine of Brahma Vidya which Shankara propounded through his works is what is known as Advaita Vedanta or Non-dualism. It confers salvation through the elimination of duality across the world.

At this time of Indian History, the spiritual life among the Buddhists was at low ebb with the vigour and purity of Buddha having vanished. The masses had moved away from the Vedic way of life comprising of the various duties in accordance with the tradition and the stages in life. A strong and urgent need for the revival of the Sanatana Dharma was therefore felt.

The Vedic rituals and sacrifices were revived and gained a position of honour. In course of time, the sacrifices and rituals *(karma kanda)* reigned supreme and were upheld as the ultimate goal. The true Vedic dictums *(jnana kanda)* were forgotten. Spiritual insight was conspicuous by its absence. At such a crucial juncture, Sri Adi Shankaracharya appeared on the scene.

Shankara realized that unless he was able to win over this powerful group of proponents and followers of ritualism, his goal of re-unifying India and making it a beacon light of spirituality would remain unfulfilled.

Thrilled by the experiences, Shankara set his mind on the task ahead and commenced his next task namely to propagate his tenets as set out in his Prasthanathraya Bhashyas to the world.

SRI SHANKARA AND KUMARILA BHATTA

Starting on this mission of a spiritual conquest of the whole of India, Shankara decided to go first to Prayag with a view to win over Kumarila, the staunch upholder of the ritualistic interpretation of the Vedas and get his explanatory comments *(Vartika)* on his Bhashya on Brahma Sutras of Badarayana – Vyasa.

Having reached Prayag, he came to know that Kumarila was about to enter into a fire, as an act of expiation for betraying his teacher from whom he had learnt stealthily the tenets of Buddhism. Sri Shankara rushed to the place where Kumarila had set himself to burn. Kumarila recognised Shankara, narrated to him his work against the Buddhists, his awareness about Sri Shankara's Bhashyas and his desire to write a Vartika (explanatory treatise) on his Bhashyas. Kumarila explained how he was not in a position to break his vow of expiation and therefore asked him to meet his disciple Mandana Misra. He added that if Shankara could defeat Mandana Misra, whose actual name was Vishwaroopa, who was the most renowned protagonist of the Purvamimamsa School, the ritualistic interpretation of the Vedas, it would clear all obstacles in the mission that Shankara had undertaken. Shankara then proceeded to Mandana's place called Mahishmati, in the present-day Bihar. (According to another version it is at the confluence of the Narmada and Mahishmati rivers, near Omkarnath in Madhya Pradesh.)

SRI SHANKARA AND MANDANA MISRA

Mandana Misra received the best of traditional training at the feet of Kumarila Bhatta and perfected his scholarship. He settled at Mahishmatipura as a householder with his wife Ubhaya Bharati.

Mandana Misra and Ubhaya Bharati were an ideal couple, each of them equal to the other in all branches of learning, ethical character and strict observation of Vedic injunctions. Ubhaya Bharati was supposed to be an avatara of goddess of learning, Saraswati Devi, as Mandana Misra was supposed to be an avatara of Brahma. His scholarship and the reverence in which he was held earned him the honorific epithet of 'Mandana Misra'. His real name was Vishwaroopa.

Mandana Misra was a distinguished practitioner of the mimamsa philosophy. The mimamsa philosophy is mainly derived from the karma kanda portion of the Vedas and emphasizes on the importance of rituals. In this school of thought, a particular ritual is done, and the results are achieved instantaneously. It displays a straightforward cause and effect relationship if practiced accurately.

When Sri Bhagavatpada reached the mansion of Mandana Misra, it was found bolted from inside. Sri Bhagavatpada, as a Sanyasin, had no right of admission into a house found closed. Such are the rules of Smriti, which govern the daily conduct of traditional Sanyasis. Sri Bhagavatpada pondered a little. He had firmly decided to redeem Mandana Misra from the rigidity of dogmatic ritualism. Therefore, he felt like using his extraordinary Yogic powers. Great Yogi and Siddha Purusha as he was, Sri Bhagavatpada entered the house through the closed door.

Mandana Misra had an innate dislike for Sanyasis because in his staunch belief of ritualism, he felt that only those who wished to escape the rigours of Vedic injunctions found a refuge in the Sanyasa ashrama. Moreover, when Sri Bhagavatpada entered the house, it was a time when the presence of a Sanyasin was most unwelcome. Mandana Misra was performing a shraddha and the Brahmins were about to be fed. The entry of Sri Bhagavatpada at such a time caused a disturbance and Mandana Misra was infuriated.

Hot and harsh exchanges followed. The Brahmins found the situation going out of control. They wished to set it right. They suggested to Mandana Misra to invite Sri Bhagavatpada for Biksha seeing him as a *bhokta* occupying Vishnu Sthana in the ceremony. Staunch ritualist as he was, Mandana Misra was fully bent upon saving the ritual. He invited Sri Bhagavatpada accordingly.

But Sri Bhagavatpada declined to accept the invitation. He explained to Mandana Misra that he did not come for *bhiksha* of the edibiles but for a *vada bhiksha*, a polemical debate in philosophy. Mandana Misra who had never met his match in learning before was willing for a dialectical fight. He gladly welcomed it. The shraddha was allowed to be finished as ordained. The debate was fixed for the next day.

Mandana Misra was a perfect and adept ritualist who preached widely. The young and charming advaita vedantin, Adi Shankara, on his country wide tour was eager to debate with Mandana Misra, who was by then already very old. Mandana Misra reasoned that since he had spent more than half his life learning and preaching mimamsa, it would be unfair to debate with a youngster in his twenties who barely had any experience. Hence, with the intention of being fair on Shankara, Misra allowed Shankara to choose his own judge. Shankara had heard greatly about Misra's righteousness and appreciated him for his act of fairness. But he was quick to decide that none but Mandana Misra's wife herself can be the most appropriate judge for this debate. To make the dispute more purposeful, they agreed to a wager. If Shankara loses in the debate, he would become a disciple of Mandana Misra and get married in this life. If Manadana Misra loses, he would become Sanyasi and disciple of Shankara. This was the bet of the debate.

The debate between them commenced and continued for months. Thousands of scholars gathered every day to watch and learn. Mandana Misra, at a ripe old age, still remained a man with very sharp intellect and a very solid grasp of logic, but he was slowly losing. Despite being such a young man, Shankara's realization of the ultimate Brahman and his knowledge of Maya, enabled him to win over Misra's arguments easily. Misra was a very accomplished ritualist, yet he seemed to lack some understanding of higher spiritual truths that Shankara seemed to have experienced already. At the end of a long period, Mandana Misra was almost ready to accept defeat, when his wife, Ubhaya Bharati, declared that in order to defeat a man in debate the opponent should also defeat his wife.

The transformation of her husband into a sannayasi distressed Bharati to no end. Wise and prudent as she was, she kept her counsel and addressed Shankara thus: "You do know that the sacred texts enjoin that a wife forms one-half of a husband's body (*ardhangini: ardha -* half; *angini* - body). Therefore, by defeating my lord, you have but won over only half of him. Your victory can be complete only when you engage in debate with me also and manage to prove yourself better."

Ubhaya Bharati was a learned scholar herself and a very clever one at that. Knowing very well that Shankara was a strict celibate, she asked him how can a sanyasi, who has no experience as a citizen, and a householder, claim complete knowledge? She immediately started discussing relationships and marital obligations. Shankara confessed that he had absolutely no knowledge in this area, because he was a celibate Sannyasi. However, Ubhaya Bharati felt that she should give Shankara some time to study about this topic before resuming the debate. Shankara immediately accepted the offer and left to start his studies.

Through his yogic powers Shankara came to know of a certain king who was about to die. He instructed his disciples to preserve his body, which he temporarily left to enter the dying king's body. The king happened to be a very evil man. Yet his wives were loyal to him and were in tears when the king was in his deathbed. Suddenly, when the king's body woke up, one of the wives noticed that the king had recovered under rather mysterious circumstances and appeared to have become a changed man.

Shankara learnt from that woman, all that he needed to know about man-woman relationship and experiences. On his way out of the body he blessed that lady who had taught him so much. Empowered with this newfound knowledge, Shankara returned to resume the debate with Ubhaya Bharati. This time, he was clearly unbeatable. Ubhaya Bharati and Mandana Misra bowed their heads in humility and accepted defeat and became followers of Adi Shankara and staunch vedantins.

Mandana Misra was given Sanyasa diksha and was given name "Sureshwara". Shankara imparted to Mandana Misra the Mahavakya 'Tat tvam asi'. Shankara having thus brought the celebrated Mandana into his own fold started again on his mission.

Sri Sureshwaracharya was the most talented disciple of Shankara Bhagavatpada. He was placed as the First Head of Sringeri Sharada Peetham in the South, one of the Mutts established by Shankara. He was the greatest scholar after Shankara in those times. He was elder to

Shankara in age. He is also called as "Vartikacharya." He wrote commentary on Shankara's Brahma Sutra Bhashyam, Dakshina Murthy Stotram.

Ubhaya Bharathi wanted to finish her *avatara* and go back to her abode. Shankara prays to her and requests her to bless people on earth. It is Ubhaya Bharathi who is considered to be blessing the devotees as Sharadamba from Sringeri.

GIST OF THE GREAT DEBATE

As the debate between Mandana Misra and Shankara, the two great stalwarts lasted for a very long duration its content is very wide in its spread and deep in its treatment. The following is the gist of these mammoth discussions.

Initiating the debate Shankara put forward the unity of all existence as follows. "Brahman, the Existence-Consciousness- Bliss Absolute (*sat-chit-ananda ghanam*) is the one ultimate Truth. It is He who appears as the entire world of multiplicity owing to dense ignorance, just as a shell appears as a piece of silver. Just as, when the illusion is dispelled, the silver is sublated by, and dissolved into its substratum, the shell, so too, when ignorance is erased, the whole world is sublated and dissolved into the substratum, Brahman, which is the same as one's own Atman. This is supreme knowledge as well as liberation. It brings about cessation of future births. The Upanishads which form the crown of the Vedas are the authority in support of this proposition. I am sure to prove this and be victorious in the debate.

If, however, I am defeated, I shall cease to be a Sanyasin, abandon the ochre robes, and assume the white dress. Let Ubhaya Bharati be the umpire to determine success or failure."

In reply to this statement, Mandana Misra made his contention as follows. "The Vedantas or the Upanishads cannot be a proof of something which is intangible i.e. Pure Consciousness, unoriginated and infinite, which has no subject-object distinguishing feature. For words can reveal only objects which are originated entities but never an abstract feature called Consciousness. Therefore, the non-vedantic part of the Vedas dealing with effects produced by works i.e. *karma kanda* is the real verbal testimony. In the light of performance of the actions in the form of rituals alone are the steps leading to *moksha* or liberation. If I happen to be defeated in argument, I shall take to the life of Sanyasa. As requested by you let my wife, Ubhaya Bharati, be the judge for the contest".

Agreeing to the conditions put forward by each other, the contestants started the debate witnessed by the learned sages and even celestials. Quoting from the Vedas as their authority and supported by enlightened arguments the debate went on for several days.

The arguments became keener and more complex, and the refutations and denials also became correspondingly stronger and bolder. Both the contestants raised more and more intricate questions. There was a downpour of assertions and objections from either side. Quotations from the scriptures were marshalled with marvellous skill by both and exploited to lend support to their case. And the debate went on. Neither side could humble the other.

The Acharya-Mandana dialogue was of such eloquence, scholarship and profundity that even the Gods assembled over Mandana's house and from above, remaining hidden from view, listened attentively to the debate. In this way, the debate was carried on for several days. As the days went by, Mandana started finding it difficult to maintain his position and give proper replies to Shankara's objections. Thereupon, Mandana, instead of defending his thesis, commenced attacking Advaita doctrine expounded in the Upanishads as put forward by Shankara. The sum and substance of the objections and the replies of the rivals are as under.

Both Mandana and Shankara accept the authority of the Vedas as the revelation standing for the ultimate good of man. Mandana's school (*Purva Mimamsa*) holds that the only purpose of the Veda is to prompt man to actions i.e. rituals sanctioned by the Veda by performance of which man attains heavenly felicity of long duration at the end of which he returns to earth – again to acquire more merits by performing *karmas.* So, the real nature of the Veda is of the nature of the commandments to actions of a ritualistic nature. If there are purely descriptive passages in it, these are descriptions of certain aids to karma like its ingredients, agents required or eulogy of the rituals etc. All such passages are to be considered as subordinate to the commandments instituting rituals. Thus, the whole of the Veda is an injunction for performance of rituals and if this is not accepted, the Veda becomes mere trash, a purposeless literature.

Contrary to this view are the views of *Uttara-mimamsakas* (Vedantins) led by Shankara. They contend that the Veda has two sections – *karma kanda* (ritualistic section) and *jnana kanda* (philosophic or knowledge section). The latter is the crown of the Veda. What the ritualists say is true of only the karma kanda and not of the Veda as a whole. The *jnana kanda* consisting of the Upanishads (also known as Vedanta) reveal the real or the ultimate meaning of the Veda and the *karma kanda* portions are merely preparatory to this. Therefore, to extend the philosophy of ritualism to the understanding of the Upanishads is a great blasphemy. The statements of the Upanishads are not commandments for any action but revelations of the nature of the Ultimate Reality and man's relation to it. They are an end in themselves and not aids to the performance of any ritual. The understanding conveyed by them releases man from the false sense of duality and establishes him in the experience of the Unity of all existence (*advaitam*: non-duality) thus releasing him for ever from the repetitive process of births and deaths (*samsara)* by rousing in him the sense of oneness with Eternal Bliss".

To put briefly, for Mandana and his school of thought Veda is revelation teaching and prompting man to perform efficacious rituals to get perishable felicities while for Shankara and his school of followers the same revelation of the Veda is a philosophy, an understanding of which establishes him in Eternal Bliss, the unity of all existence, *moksha* or liberation. Ubhaya Bharati, the umpire, accepted the cogent arguments of Shankara and overruled the contentions of Mandana Misra thereby defeating him, her own husband. The rest was history as already described.

CONCLUSION

From the foregoing account of the discussion the following facts emerge.

1. Quoting various authorities and supporting the same with weighty arguments the contest was conducted in a highly dignified manner producing more light than heat, the contestants showing due respect to each other.

2. Women were held in high esteem and noted for their scholarship and erudition and more so because of their impartiality and fair-mindedness.

3. The *guru-shishya* relationship between Shankara and Sureshwara proves the dictum in the Dakshina Murthy Stotram that a Guru can be young and a Shishya can be old and that such association has got nothing to do with age of the persons concerned.

With our world in the Kaliyugam battling a crisis of identities, gender and grappling with intellectual ideas of inclusivity, I will leave you with the Nishkama Shatakam, a gem of a composition by Adi Shankaracharya himself to help us transcend what we are not and attain what we truly are:

Nirvana Shatakam Lyrics and Meaning

Nirvana Shatakam, composed by Adi Shankara himself, embodies the spiritual pursuit. Here are the lyrics and meaning of this timeless composition.

mano buddhi ahankara chittani naaham

na cha shrotravjihve na cha ghraana netre

na cha vyoma bhumir na tejo na vaayuhu

chidananda rupah shivo'ham shivo'ham

I am not any aspect of the mind like the intellect, the ego or the memory,

I am not the organs of hearing, tasting, smelling or seeing,

I am not the space, nor the earth, nor fire, nor air, I am the form of consciousness and bliss, am Shiva (that which is not)...

na cha prana sangyo na vai pancha vayuhu

na va sapta dhatur na va pancha koshah

na vak pani-padam na chopastha payu

chidananda rupah shivo'ham shivo'ham

I am not the Vital Life Energy (Prana), nor the Five Vital Airs (manifestations of Prana),

I am not the seven essential ingredients nor the 5 sheaths of the body, I am not any of the body parts, like the mouth, the hands, the feet, etc.,

I am the form of consciousness and bliss, I am Shiva (that which is not)...

na me dvesha ragau na me lobha mohau

na me vai mado naiva matsarya bhavaha

na dharmo na chartho na kamo na mokshaha

chidananda rupah shivo'ham shivo'ham

There is no hatred nor passion in me, no greed nor delusion,

There is no pride, nor jealousy in me,

I am not identified with my duty, wealth, lust or liberation, I am the form of consciousness and bliss, I am Shiva (that which is not)...

na punyam na papam na saukhyam na duhkham

na mantro na tirtham na veda na yajnah

aham bhojanam naiva bhojyam na bhokta

chidananda rupah shivo'ham shivo'ham

I am not virtue nor vice, not pleasure or pain,

I need no mantras, no pilgrimage, no scriptures or rituals,

I am not the experience, not the object of experience, not even the one who experiences,

I am the form of consciousness and bliss, I am Shiva (that which is not)....

na me mrtyu shanka na mejati bhedaha

pita naiva me naiva mataa na janmaha

na bandhur na mitram gurur naiva shishyaha

chidananda rupah shivo'ham shivo'ham

I am not bound by death and its fear, not by caste or creed,

I have no father, nor mother, or even birth,

I am not a relative, nor a friend, nor a teacher nor a student, I am the form of consciousness and bliss, am Shiva (that which is not)...

aham nirvikalpo nirakara rupo

vibhut vatcha sarvatra sarvendriyanam

na cha sangatham naiva muktir na meyaha

chidananda rupah shivo'ham shivo'ham

I am devoid of duality, my form is formlessness,

I am omnipresent, I exist everywhere, pervading all senses,

I am neither attached, neither free nor limited, I am the form of consciousness and bliss, I am Shiva (that which is not)...

If you found value in this book, please pass it on to other Hindus to read and recommend / review it on Amazon. I promise not to keep a single rupee from proceeds (Author Earnings I receive from the Publisher) after taxes and will keep donating the proceeds for Dharmic causes. My objective is to unite ALL Hindus of Bharath and world over and support and educate ALL Hindus and those protecting our Dharma monetarily and with my limited knowledge.

कायेन वाचा मनसेन्द्रियैर्वा ।

बुद्ध्यात्मना वा प्रकृतेः स्वभावात् ।

करोमि यद्यत्सकलं परस्मै ।

नारायणयेति समर्पयामि ॥

Kaayena Vaacaa Manase[a-I]ndriyair-Vaa

Buddhy[i]-Aatmanaa Vaa Prakrteh Svabhaavaat |

Karomi Yad-Yat-Sakalam Parasmai

Naaraayannnayeti Samarpayaami ||

Meaning:

1. (Whatever I do) with my Body, Speech, Mind or Sense Organs,
2. ... or using my Intellect, Feelings of Heart or (unconsciously) through the natural tendencies of my Mind,
3. All those, I do for the Supreme Being (without sense of attachment to the results),
4. (And) I Surrender them to the Lotus Feet of Sri Narayana.

I also seek forgiveness from the Almighty Paramatma and my Gurus, if due to my ignorance or lack of knowledge, I have said anything wrong or against our

Dharma by oversight. Please forgive me as I am still learning and have miles to go before I understand the depth of wisdom that is Sanatana Dharma.

Koti Koti Pranams to my Gurus without whose spiritual guidance I would have never been able to even start writing this book, let alone finish and publish it:

Above is a picture I took of my Guru HH Jagadguru Vijayendra Saraswati Swamigal (Bala Periyava) after he gave me permission to write this book. I love him dearly and yearn to be under his benign grace all the time.

So much of the knowledge in this book is from Paramacharya (Mahaperiyava) HH Jagadguru Chandrashekarendra Saraswati Swamigal who blessed me with a shall before my Upanayanam many moons ago when I was 13 years old and was clueless about the sheer spiritual power of the great man (God himself). I know for a fact that he has guided me in writing this book in more ways than one. He was literally God in human form and guides me and so many devotees in spirit even today:

I also humbly prostrate to HH Jagadguru Jayendra Saraswati Swamigal who has done yeoman service to Sanatana Dharma and his Ashirvadams every time I have gone for Darshan when he was in his physical body:

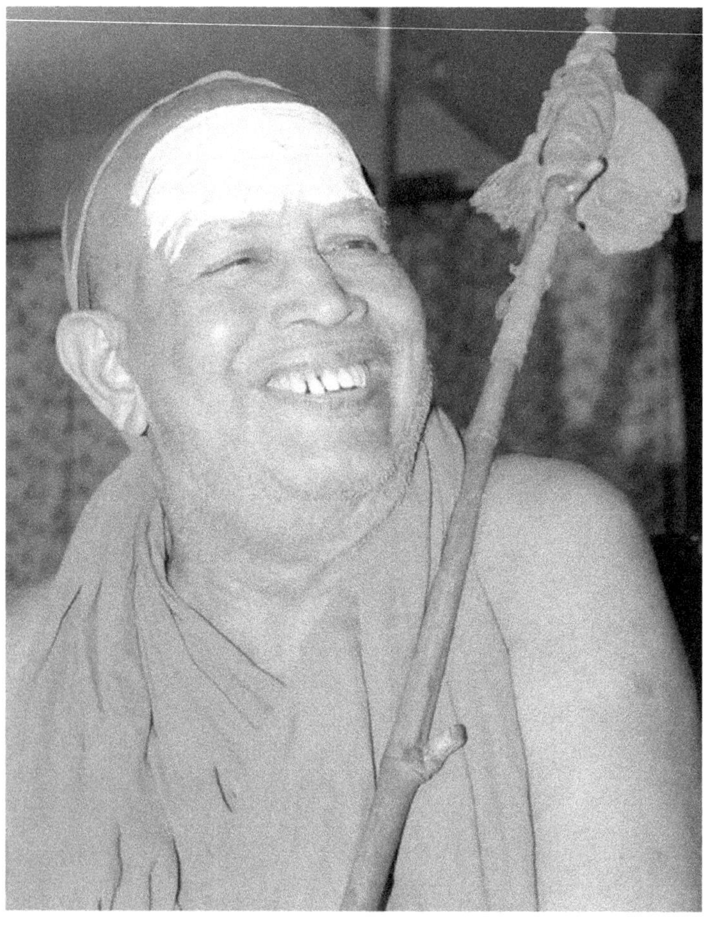

REFERENCES

Hindu Dharma by Jagadguru Shri Chandrasekharendra Saraswati Mahaswamigal

Works of Swami Vivekananda

Various books about HH Ramana Maharishi

Autobiography of a Yogi by Paramahamsa Yogananda

Voice of God speeches and thoughts of Shri Chandrasekharendra Saraswati Mahaswamigal

https://www.scientificamerican.com/article/consciousness-is-a-continuum-and-scientists-are-starting-to-measure-it/

https://hbr.org/2020/04/the-restorative-power-of-ritual

https://www.grander.com/intl-en/international/grander-water/water-research/basic-research/the-element-water/fun-facts/water-has-a-memory

https://mahaperiyavaa.blog/2016/08/02/pray-6-times-a-day/

https://www.wikihow.com/Perform-the-Tahajjud-Prayer

https://curlytales.com/womens-only-temples-in-india-where-men-are-not-allowed/

https://arvind-bhagwath.medium.com/why-are-all-the-major-shiva-temples-in-india-almost-along-a-straight-line-54a3107bb857

Quora answer by Snehashis Mohanta who is a B. A in Social Issues in India & Politics, Ravenshaw University, Cuttack about whether Sati had any Vedic, religious significance at all:

https://en.wikipedia.org/wiki/79th_meridian_east

Madhyarekha, Madhyarekhā, Madhya-rekha: 2 definitions

https://en.wikipedia.org/wiki/Siddh%C4%81nta_Shiromani

https://en.wikipedia.org/wiki/Omphalos)

https://en.wikipedia.org/wiki/Axis_mundi

https://en.wikipedia.org/wiki/Circumambulation

https://en.wikipedia.org/wiki/Brihadisvara_Temple,_Thanjavur

https://en.wikipedia.org/wiki/Surya_Siddhanta

https://ancientstarmyths.blogspot.com/

https://en.wikipedia.org/wiki/Sanchita_karma#:~:text=In%20Hinduism%2C%20Sanchita%20karma%20(heaped,are%20stored%20in%20one's%20subconscious.

https://en.wikipedia.org/wiki/Karma_in_Hinduism#:~:text=There%20are%20three%20different%20types,of%20current%20decisions%20and%20actions.

https://youtu.be/H8ImcskQqwM?feature=shared

Varamihira: https://shyamasundaradasa.com/jyotish/resources/articles/varaha_mihira.html#:~:text=Going%20into%20meditation%20after%20studying,the%20prince%20from%20the%20jaws

https://en.wikipedia.org/wiki/Angus_Maddison_statistics_of_the_ten_largest_economies_by_GDP_(PPP)

https://www.facebook.com/ZeeNewsEnglish/videos/dna-know-the-history-of-aurangzebs-atrocities-on-hindus/565053964759198/

https://www.opindia.com/2022/03/rani-naiki-devi-a-brave-queen-of-chalukyas-who-defeated-muhammad-ghori/

https://ramanisblog.in/2017/10/23/tipu-massacred-800-mandyam-brahmins-melkote-on-deepavali/

https://www.jagranjosh.com/general-knowledge/rani-lakshmibai-biography-1592467437-1

https://www.youtube.com/watch?v=2KOw_R5s5Qc&t=7s

https://dharmawiki.org/index.php/Kshatriya_Dharma_(%E0%A4%95%E0%A5%8D%E0%A4%B7%E0%A4%A4%E0%A5%8D%E0%A4%B0%E0%A4%BF%E0%A4%AF%E0%A4%A7%E0%A4%B0%E0%A5%8D%E0%A4%AE%E0%A4%83)

Shudra Rulers https://www.jstor.org/stable/44138596

https://isha.sadhguru.org/en/wisdom/article/body-memories-washing-of-runanubandha

https://isha.sadhguru.org/en/blog/article/nirvana-shatakam-lyrics-meaning

https://www.esamskriti.com/e/Spirituality/Vedanta/The-classic-debate-between-Mandana-Misra-and-Adi-Shankara-1.aspx

https://vedictruth.blogspot.com/2016/11/vedas-and-sati-pratha.html

Dr. Anadi Sahoo's research and posts

https://www.indiatoday.in/science/story/big-bang-didn-t-start-our-universe-there-was-another-universe-before-it-nobel-laureate-roger-penrose-1730064-2020-10-09

Text from YouTube Channel : Social Vaani

https://www.linkedin.com/posts/dranadisahoo_navagraha-navgraha-navagrahahomam-activity-7212004924342030336-veEl/?utm_source=share&utm_medium=member_android

esamskriti.com.

then only will one feel its warmth. This is the part of my job that gives me the most pleasure and satisfaction. Teaching is a vocation, not just a profession...it takes over one's every waking moment....and there's nothing else I would rather do!

Warm wishes and hugs,
Periwinkle

Epilogue

In the words of Daniel Webster, who motivates me to be an 'educator with purpose'...

'If we work upon marble, it will perish;

If we work upon brass, time will efface it; If we rear monuments,

They can crumble to dust.

But if we work upon immortal minds...

If we imbue them with high principles, awe of God and love of their fellowmen,

We engrave on those tablets,

Something which no time can efface, but Which will brighten all eternity'.

**Warm wishes and hugs,
Periwinkle**

Thank you to…

My husband, L, for always pushing me to keep going, holding my hand when I lost focus and believing in what I have to say.

My children who think I am 'the best mum in the world'!

Notion Press publishing house... and their whole team.

I would not have got this done if it wasn't for you.

Warm wishes and hugs,
Periwinkle